MULTILATERAL TREATY-MAKING

NIJHOFF LAW SPECIALS

VOLUME 47

The titles published in this series are listed at the end of this volume.

The American Society
of International Law

The Graduate Institute
of International Studies

Multilateral Treaty-Making

The Current Status of Challenges to and Reforms Needed in the International Legislative Process

Papers presented at the Forum Geneva
held in Geneva, Switzerland
May 16, 1998

Edited by
Vera Gowlland-Debbas

With the Assistance of
Hassiba Hadj-Sahraoui and Nobuo Hayashi

MARTINUS NIJHOFF PUBLISHERS
THE HAGUE / BOSTON / LONDON

A C.I.P. Catalogue record for this book is available from the Library of Congress.

ISBN 90-411-1448-3

Published by Kluwer Law International,
P.O. Box 85889, 2508 CN The Hague, The Netherlands.

Sold and distributed in North, Central and South America
by Kluwer Law International,
675 Massachusetts Avenue, Cambridge, MA 02139, U.S.A.

In all other countries, sold and distributed
by Kluwer Law International,
P.O. Box 85889, 2508 CN The Hague, The Netherlands.

Cover:
Suyderhoef, Jonas, after Gerard ter Borch
The 'swearing of the oath of ratification' of the peace of Münster,
in the main hall of the town hall of Münster, 1648.
Frederik Muller 1941, engraving and etching
Rijksmuseum-Stichting Amsterdam

Printed on acid-free paper

Printed in the Netherlands.

Table of Contents

Foreword

The American Society of International Law and the Graduate Institute of International Studies wish to thank the Republic National Bank of New York (Suisse), the Société Suisse de Droit International and its President, Professor Walter Kälin, and the Programme for the Study of International Organizations (PSIO), GIIS, and its Executive Director, Dr. Daniel Warner, for their financial support in organizing Forum Geneva.

The Program Organizing Committee was composed of Mahnoush H. Arsanjani, United Nations, New York, and Vera Gowlland-Debbas, GIIS, with the collaboration of Charlotte Ku, Executive Director, ASIL. Special thanks go to Sandra Liebel, ASIL, Isabelle Gerardi, GIIS, and Lisa Krahenbuhl, PSIO, for their organization of the Forum.

VERA GOWLLAND-DEBBAS

Introductory Remarks

The contributions in this book on multilateral treaty-making emerged from Forum Geneva, held jointly by the American Society of International Law and the Graduate Institute of International Studies in Geneva on May 16, 1998.

The subtitle, "The Current Status of Challenges to, and Reforms Needed in, the International Legislative Process", indicates that multilateral treaty-making has not been examined in a static sense, but placed against the backdrop of the interaction between international legal system and social change. There is no need for any reminder of the vast political, economic, social and technological transformations which have taken place and are still in process in this past decade, although I will refrain from all references to globalization in this context. (In fact, the Forum proceedings took place against the noisy background of anti-WTO demonstrators.)

But there are of course different ways of envisaging this exchange between law and society. One can envisage the legal system as a kind of self-contained black box containing a coherently ordered set of structural and normative arrangements, the systemic character of which can be conceptualized in various ways, such as in the formalist terms of Kelsen's linear pyramidal structure, for whom the fundamental norm serves as a boundary between the legal system and its extra-systemic social environment, or Herbert Hart's union between primary and secondary rules. Within this self-regulating system, law provides its own means of validation (or its sources or rules of recognition) and sanctions violations of its binding norms. From this perspective the international lawyer need not be overly concerned with social change.

One can on the other hand view international law as instrumental, there to promote certain finalities and/or underlying values and interests. From this perspective, the legal system becomes synonymous with the notion of legal order, in the sense of a particular substantive content surfacing at any one time and hence dynamic in the sense of responding to the changing configuration and requirements of the component parts of international society.

It has been pointed out that it is particularly at a time of growing divergence between social mores and legal institutions that doctrine tends to approach the in-

V. Gowlland-Debbas (ed.), Multilateral Treaty-making, 1–9.

ternational legal system as open-ended, empirically and sociologically based, interrelating with other disciplines and with social reality itself. While Kelsen's insistence on the strict autonomy of the law may have taken place in reaction to the brutal transformations of the social order of his time, and in some way constitute an attempt to save the law from destruction through its instrumentalization, it is interesting to note that he was at the same time, well aware of the dilemma created by his postulate of the complete separation of jurisprudence from politics:[1]

> "This is especially true in our time, which indeed 'is out of joint' when the foundations of social life have been shaken to the depths by two World Wars. The ideal of an objective science of law and State, free from all political ideologies, has a better chance for recognition in a period of social equilibrium. It seems, therefore, that a pure theory of law is untimely today. . . ."

Nevertheless, the interrelationship between law and society is a complex one, for the international legal system does not transform everything into law; it is in this way that law succeeds in preserving its detachment from the disturbance emanating from society. In short, law ingests only those legally relevant facts which are to be attributed legal consequences (e.g. State practice, or State will), defining the threshold of normativity that must be crossed. From this viewpoint, law has the paradoxical position of being both open to its international environment with its sociological, political, moral or economic foundations, and closed, because these are reinterpreted according to a specifically legal matrix.

Speaking of thresholds of normativity leads us to the focus of our Forum, that is the rules of recognition, or if one prefers, the sources of international law, more particularly those rules relating to the mode of production and change of the normative system through multilateral treaties, which have been codified in the triptych on treaties – the 1969 Vienna Convention on the Law of Treaties, the unratified 1986 Vienna Convention on the Law of Treaties between States and International Organizations or between International Organizations, and the 1978 Vienna Convention on Succession of States in Respect of Treaties which has recently entered into force.

It must be emphasized therefore that this collection of contributions on multilateral treaty-making focuses on the *instrumentum*, the instrument in which the international obligations are expressed, and not on the *negotium* or content of the agreements themselves, and therefore on the impact of social change on the rules relating to forms and procedures of treaty-making. Yet inevitably, we come to focus on the content, for in certain areas such as human rights or the environment, it is the substance of the norms themselves that have had an impact on the form and procedure of the treaty.

---

1 Hans Kelsen, *General Theory of Law and State* (Translated by Anders Wedberg) (Harvard University Press, Cambridge, Mass., 1945), p. xvii.

Beginning from the classical elements of the definition of a treaty – "an international agreement concluded between subjects of international law, governed by international law, whatever its particular designation" – I would like to raise the following questions, which in part cut across the panels.

IS MULTILATERAL TREATY-MAKING THE MOST APPROPRIATE TOOL FOR MEETING THE NEW NEEDS AND REQUIREMENTS OF CURRENT INTERNATIONAL SOCIETY?

Roberto Ago once wrote: "La prise de conscience du besoin de procéder à une codification est pratiquement toujours allée de pair, dans l'Histoire, avec la survenance de la nécessité de codifier, dans une mesure parfois très profonde et rapide, le droit existant au sein d'une société où s'était produit un changement révolutionnaire des structures sociales ou, en tout cas, une transformation radicale de la composition de la société."[2]

This recalls the process of decolonization which had produced tremendous changes in the international environment, both quantitatively in increasing the number of nation-States and qualitatively in changing patterns of interests and claims, and the resulting impact on the sources of international law created by the new States emerging from this process. Requestioning the traditional Eurocentric content of international law elaborated by a small minority of States, the "new" States had called for greater participation in the legal system and more programmatory law better suited to an increasingly heterogeneous and interdependent society, emphasizing both reinforcement of State sovereignty and newly insisted upon State solidarity. This was reflected in their great suspicion of the customary law process and their resort both to the United Nations General Assembly majority voting system as the best instrument for advancing their claims and to multilateral treaty-making in which they could act on the basis of sovereign equality. The result was vast efforts in codification: whether in the form of non-binding General Assembly resolutions and codes of conduct, or in the development of major areas of international law through the great diplomatic law-making conferences. Texts were thus adopted through consensus or majority votes, obtained by a process of compromise, bargaining and package-deals (as for example the 1982 United Nations Convention on the Law of the Sea), although this could and did lead in some cases to subsequent difficulties in ratification or impasse on implementation.

We find ourselves once again in a changed world environment in which the components of international society have been altered both quantitatively as a result of the break up of the Soviet Union and other States in Eastern Europe and qualitatively in the sense of raising new legal claims which in turn have required

---

[2] Roberto Ago, "Nouvelles réflexions sur la codification du droit international" (1988) 92 RGDIP, pp. 539-576.

addressing new legal issues demanding codification, as for example, those resulting from State succession, assertion of minority rights and ethnic strife.

In so far as codification and progressive development is concerned, the 50th birthday of the International Law Commission has led to stock-taking over its role. How has this body of experts addressed the question of meeting new needs? The relationship between the ILC and the Sixth Committee reflects the relationship between the legal and the political, but to what extent should new demands emanating from the political body be reflected in the work of the ILC? It is clear that the ILC is in part, sensitive to the changing political climate, not least by virtue of a representation which is not intended to be, but has become, increasingly more diplomatic, and in this sense, as Alain Pellet points out in his Keynote Address on "Responding to New Needs through Codification and Progressive Development", it undermines the complementarity between the expert body and its political counterpart. One can recall in this context, the shift in conceptualization of State responsibility under the impact of the developing and socialist countries, from its original focus on the primary rules relating to State responsibility for injury to aliens reflecting First World concerns over protection of foreign investment, to a focus on the secondary rules encompassing all the legal consequences of unlawful acts; the controversy over State crimes and countermeasures, reflects also certain political tensions between powerful and less powerful States. However, Alain Pellet shows us that the ILC cannot address purely and simply all political claims. Its role, in his view, is not to legislate; law has its limits, and some issues requiring technical expertise or which are politically sensitive are not ripe for codification by that expert body. He advocates rather a role relegated to meeting not new needs but the *real* needs of international society; one, in other words, which addresses its constitutional structure, for "a slowly consolidating international society needs uniform legal rules which transversally cut through all fields covered by international law" bridging over the technicalities and specializations. But codification does not necessarily mean binding instruments: ILC drafts have been made use of by the International Court of Justice, and its work on reservations to treaties may well adopt the flexible form of a declaration.

In his lunchtime address on "The International Treaty-Making Process: Paradise Lost, or Humpty Dumpty?", Charles Brower reminds us however of the current reticence of certain States *vis-à-vis* multilateral treaty-making, who prefer to pick and choose from the content of international law on the basis of customary international law. I would add to the examples he gives, the recent cases of the 1997 UN Convention on Anti-personnel Mines and the 1998 Rome Statute of the International Criminal Court, in which the refusal to join of one State, the United States, despite its participation in the negotiating process and the securing of some of its goals, raises the potential effects which this may have on the treaties' implementation. What is the answer? Brower advocates some privatization of the international lawmaking process, more elaboration of purely customary law, or different approaches to treaty-making, such as so-called "framework" conventions, which he considers may address some of these problems. The point which should

Standard-Setting Action: International Legislation or Treaty Law?" presents arguments in favour of the quasi-legislative character of international labour conventions arising from the treaty-making process itself. This arises from legislative interpretation of conventions, the ruling out of reservations, and the creation of a fairly integrated single "legislative corpus", as opposed to interpretation of conventions in isolation. The International Labour Conference, he points out, has become an organ capable of adopting and repealing international legislation. Conventions have thus become legal tools whose "raison d'être is subordinated to the more general and fundamental objectives spelled out in the Constitution".

In his Concluding Remarks, Georges Abi-Saab focuses on three axes of multilateral treaty-making: its process, fora, and outcome. He points as well to two sources of complexity: "the multiplicity of actions and the heterogeneity of subject-matters". The dilemma, in the final analysis, is, in his words: "how to accommodate the increasing demand for, and trend towards diversity with the imperative of preserving the unity of the international legal system".

Multilateral Treaties as a Source of International Law

Chair: LARRY JOHNSON

ALAIN PELLET

Responding to New Needs through Codification and Progressive Development

KEYNOTE ADDRESS

I have been assigned the formidable honour of presenting a "keynote address" on the general theme of this Forum, "Multilateral Treaty-Making". This is, indeed, formidable since this theme is not only extremely vast but already largely explored – if only by the two quite stimulating colloquiums organized on the occasion of the fiftieth anniversary of the International Law Commission in New York in October 1997[1] and in Geneva in April 1998.[2] The danger then is that I am afraid that I will not be able to escape the commonplace and platitudes – although this may be what is expected in a "keynote address".

Another danger is that in presenting a superficial overview I may be anticipating the various topics which will be dealt with later by infinitely more qualified speakers.

However, I must say, it is a great privilege: coming first leaves you freer to speak of whatever you have in mind, although there is the risk of breaking into the following speakers' topics. I have tried to avoid this and it has not proved too difficult since, being a specialist of nothing, I am definitely not a specialist in the various fields which will be explored later on by eminent experts in all the fields represented in our very substantial programme which will surely satisfy your intellectual appetite. I can, therefore, prudently avoid speaking about the topic which was assigned to me and, at the risk of simply repeating what is no secret to this distin-

---

[1] *Making Better International Law – The International Law Commission at 50 (Proceedings of the United Nations Colloquium on Progressive Development and Codification of International Law*, (United Nations, New York, 1998), Sales n° E/F.98.V.5, XI–451 pp.

[2] International Law Commission, Round-Table Discussions, April 22-28 1998, to be published by the United Nations, 2000. See also M. R. Anderson *et al.* (eds.), *The International Law Commission and the Future of International Law*, (British Institute of International and Comparative Law, Public International Law Series, London, 1998), XXI-239pp. and Société française pour le droit international, colloque d'Aix-en-Provence, *La codification du droit international*, (Pédone, Paris, 1999), 344pp.

V. Gowlland-Debbas (ed.), Multilateral Treaty-making, 13–23.

guished audience, I will confine myself mainly to generalities and to what I am familiar with, that is, the codification process through the International Law Commission, a subject which, I am afraid, is marked by a distressing taste of banality …

*

The sub-title which has been given to this presentation is: "Responding to New Needs through Codification and Progressive Development". For the reasons I have just indicated, I will add a "sub-sub-title": "Can the ILC respond?".

Both the sub-title and the sub-sub question in turn suppose that there are new needs … "New"? Compared to what? "Needs"? How do we evaluate them? And, by the way, is there a need for codification at all?

After all, the very idea of codification is relatively new in modern times. In domestic law, it was only experimented with – and not in all countries – from the French Revolution onward. At the international level, codification remained a purely doctrinal aspiration until 1930 and, if we are realistic, until the creation of the ILC fifty years ago. Yet the world had survived without a formalized codification process.

On the other hand, it can also be argued that, even though no formalized process existed, States did codify without being conscious of it, exactly as M. Jourdain, Molière's *Bourgeois gentilhomme*, was making prose without knowing it. It is not incongruous to consider that The Hague Conventions of 1899 and 1907 were, indeed, codification conventions, at least in the broad sense, since they involved an important, and probably a predominant, element of progressive development and indeed of development "*tout court*", not that much "progressive" but, better, "progress<u>ist</u>" (even though I am not sure the word exists in English … ; let's say that they involve important elements of purely revolutionary development as opposed to gradual development – and I will come back later to this point).

More generally speaking, one can wonder whether "*traités-lois*" as opposed to "*traités-contrats*" do not qualify as codification conventions in this broad meaning of the term. In my opinion, the general and non-synallagmatic character of the substantial norms included in an instrument is, no doubt, a criterion which allows one to differentiate a codification text from instruments which do not present such a character.

Is this enough? Probably not since the very idea of codification also implies an attempt to unite in a single instrument a complete *corpus juris*, a whole set of rules relevant to a given field of social relations. Just to take two examples, I would suggest that the 1928 Covenant, the so-called Briand-Kellogg Treaty, cannot be said to be a codification convention while, on the other hand, as I have said, The Hague Conventions can. Similarly, there is no doubt that the Conventions on the Law of the Sea of 1958 and 1982 belong to the codification sphere; that delimitation agreements do not; while there can be discussion regarding, say, treaties regulating fisheries in some portions of the Atlantic.

I have not yet finished with these problems of definition. Up to now, I have accepted that codification, in the broad acceptance of the term, supposes the gathering of general rules pertaining to a given topic in a single instrument. Is this enough? I would say yes; but this is not generally accepted. Two other conditions are sometimes added (and, in fact, they are more often than not):

– *first*, codification would imply the mere gathering of existing rules, as opposed to new rules forged in order to answer new or evolving needs;

– *second*, the instrument embodying the rules is sometimes seen as being necessarily binding; failing this one could only speak of tentative codification.

I am not convinced by these supposed additional requirements.

It is commonplace to recall that distinguishing between "pure" codification on the one hand and progressive development on the other hand, while intellectually attractive, has proved practically impossible. Indeed the Statute of the ILC is based on such a distinction, but it has never "worked" in practice: neither regarding the selection of topics, nor in respect of the procedure followed or the outcome of its work, has the Commission made (or been able to make) a difference between both aspects. All topics involve partial codification since no topic is entirely new when it is undertaken by the ILC (except, maybe, purely institutional matters – I refer here to the draft Statute of the International Criminal Court); in addition, all imply an element of progressive development since, almost as a matter of definition, customary rules always comprise some elements of uncertainty calling for clarification and this is precisely one of the main purposes of codification; and this is even true in very ancient fields of international relations largely regulated by well established rules, such as diplomatic or consular relations or the law of treaties.

This being said, in practice, this does not raise real difficulties; it only allows Members of the International Law Commission to make erudite speeches distinguishing between both aspects, but nothing can be inferred from this and it is usually of no consequence at all – except in those very rare cases where the Commission confers a distinct status to provisions which, in its opinion, belong to codification on the one hand, and those belonging to progressive development on the other hand. One of the rare occasions when the ILC made an attempt to make such a distinction was the draft articles on "Nationality in relation to the succession of States" adopted on first reading in 1997. In this precise case, the Commission divided its draft into two parts: Part I was devoted to "General Provisions", supposedly applicable to all categories of succession of States, while Part II consisted of "Provisions related to Specific Categories of Succession of States". However, although the Special Rapporteur, Dr. Vaclav Mikulka, had on several occasions indicated that Part I bore mainly on codification, while Part II was more "progressive development oriented", it appeared quite difficult to maintain the distinction (even if it surfaces here and there in the commentaries and in some provisions, mainly in Article 19, which introduce Part II).[3]

[3] See ILC, Report on the Work of its Forty-Ninth Session, 12 May-18 July 1997, UN Doc. GAOR Fifty-Second Session, Supp. N° 10 (A/52/10), at 72.

This shows once again how artificial the distinction is: "pure" codification constantly interferes with progressive development; there is certainly no clear threshold. Therefore, even though this conclusion would probably disappoint some learned scholars, particularly those – and they are quite numerous in academic circles ... – who are obsessed with clear and straightforward classifications, the only sensible conclusion is that progressive development is indissociable from codification; it is indeed part of codification.

Now, this purely definitional problem is not the core of the question. The real question is: when is legal development "progressive"? when is it more than that? Here again, I have no doubt that there is no clear, indisputable threshold; and there is nothing strange in that: law in general, and international law in particular, is not a "hard" science; it is an "art", *ars juris* ... But the absence of threshold, certainly does not mean that any new rule of international law qualifies as a "progressive" development.

This is extremely important in respect of the work of the ILC: we are a group of thirty-four independent experts, without any political mandate or responsibility. It would be, from my point of view, absolutely disastrous and extremely arrogant that we assume the role of a legislator; "codifiers" (here again, I doubt that the word exists in English) we are; law-makers (even quasi-legislators) we are not, except in the very rare cases where we are expressly given such a role (here again, the draft Statute of the ICC is probably the only, at least the most striking example, of such an exceptional mandate). In my mind the difference is that we may complete the existing law with *progressive* developments; we cannot change the whole system of the law of nations. Our job is "lawyers' law", not "politicians' law". I mean that it is our duty to try to understand the logic of existing rules and to develop them in the framework of this logic, not to change the underlying logic. It is our duty to keep our ears and our eyes and our mind open to the changes in the law of nations and to take note of new trends, not to invent them and certainly even less to impose them.

I know that this might seem rather conservative – and, by the way, I have no doubt that law is conservative by its very nature –, but I also think that legal development is, globally, something much too serious to be entrusted to lawyers. And this is not specific to international law: inside the State, law is made by politicians, through (at least in democratic States) Parliaments or through Governments invested with political responsibilities, not by lawyers; as Sir Robert Jennings put it, "No developed nation would allow its legislative policy to be decided upon just by the lawyers. They would be employed to advise and to draft; but the legislative policy would be decided by those who understood the matter the subject of the legislation."[4] Progressive development is the extreme limit of what is tolerable and I think that the ILC would be well inspired not to abuse the confidence placed upon it by its Statute.

---

[4] "International Law Reform and Progressive Development", in Liber Amicorum *Professor Ignaz Seidl-Hohenveldern in Honour of His 80th Birthday* (Kluwer, The Hague, 1998), p. 334.

Let me give an example: in 1994, Professor Arangio-Ruiz, the then Special Rapporteur on State Responsibility, presented an admirable report on the determination of crimes (in the meaning of Article 19 of the Draft Articles). Inspired by an eminently respectable moral ideal, he had elaborated an incredible system including recourse to the General Assembly, the Security Council and the ICJ.[5] This was admirable but, with respect, it was totally unrealistic and, to tell the truth, quite absurd: whether you like it or not, international society is not domestic society and it is of no use at all to try to transplant internal legal reasoning and institutions into the international sphere; the transplantation cannot take effect – except if it is very gradual and rooted in a political context which makes it acceptable for the community of States.

Moreover and in any case, the ILC is certainly not the appropriate forum to promote such a radical development; nor is it the right place to try to "judicialize" international society, as Part III of these same Draft Articles on State Responsibility tries to do.[6] Legal experts are not negotiators; they are not supposed to bargain or to compromise, but, once again, to codify and to develop *progressively* (that is gradually) existing law. Would the odd idea that the ILC could be the right forum to discuss the CTBT occur to the mind of any of us? Certainly not: this kind of treaty implies a huge technical expertise on an immensely complex range of problems outside the legal field, taking into account very diverse factors of a political, military and economic nature which arc out of rcach of a handful of lawyers, however eminent they may be.

It is good form, within international law circles, to deplore that the second "codification" of the law of the sea was realized outside the ILC. I would certainly not join the mourners choir! Indeed the Commission performed a respectable job in elaborating the 1958 Geneva Conventions; but, at the same time, the failure of the second Conference on the Law of the Sea in 1960 showed the limits of using a purely legal preparatory process and I am firmly convinced that the ILC would have been incapable of taking into account all the relevant data, including complex geo-political issues involved by the new developments which occurred in the rapidly changing political and economic context during the 1970s.

For the same kind of reasons, I am among those who are quite opposed to burdening the Commission with new topics such as "The General Principles of the Law of the Environment": too politically sensitive, too economically delicate, too wide, not ripe … And the precedent of the "Liability" topic is far from encouraging in this respect.

This, however, certainly does not mean that multilateral treaty-making should be confined to codification (including progressive development) in the pure sense. It simply means that not all topics are fit for the ILC or comparable forums (even

---

[5] See ILC, *Yearbook* 1994, vol. II, Part II, paras. 261-266, pp.141-42; Sixth Report on State Responsibility by Mr. Gaetano Arangio-Ruiz, Special Rapporteur, A/CN.4/461/Add.1, paras.6-8, at 4.

[6] See ILC, Report on the Work of its Forty-Eighth Session, 6 May-26 July 1996, UN Doc. GAOR Fifty-First Session, Supp. N° 10 (A/51/10), pp. 147-151.

though I feel that the ILC is rather unique and I will come back to it in a minute). If they are highly sensitive politically speaking, they must be tackled in purely political (that is, since we are in the international sphere, diplomatic) forums (with the possibility of having some preparatory work done in the ILC as shown here again, by the precedent of the Criminal Court; but it also shows that it is unavoidable that, in such a case, this work be carried on at the diplomatic level). If the issues at stake are highly technical (besides legal technicalities), the topic must be dealt with in places where this expertise is available. And, if the topic involves a mixture of political, technical and legal issues, then, something like the Third Conference on the Law of the Sea is probably unavoidable.

For the reasons I have developed, the inadequacy of the ILC in all these cases is averred even though one of the reasons for its uniqueness is the irreplaceable constant backward and forward motion between the "scientific" and the political part of the process. We, in room XXI of the Palace of Nations are, or at least should be, concerned with collecting and analyzing precedents (whether judicial or practical) and doctrinal views, assembling them with a view to ascertaining evidence of practice generally accepted as being the law and to deduce the existence of new trends, and elaborating drafts with a concern for reasonableness, consistency and acceptability – a word on which I intend to come back. They, in the Sixth Committee in New York, are (or, again, should be) concerned with determining topics which meet the needs of States and deserve attention from the Commission, with making sure that our drafts meet these needs, and with giving clear guidance to the Commission in this respect.

In practice, this does not work very satisfactorily and, in my view, the States bear the main responsibility for this unsatisfactory situation. I was in the position, in 1997, to represent the Commission that I chaired, to the Sixth Committee and I must confess that I have been rather dismayed at the stereotyped reactions of States delegates' speeches on the ILC drafts: most of the time they had not been read and, in the best cases, the speakers had contented themselves with reading the Chapter of our Report entitled "Summary of the Work of the Commission" (a new initiative we had taken in the hope that, at least, they would read something ...) or, for others (with the exceptions of representatives of some powerful States, always the same ones ...), to repeat what the first speakers had said some days ago.

Not only is this rather discouraging for the ILC, but also it is highly telling about the actual state of international relations: you have a handful of Western Powers, efficiently organized, where the job is done and whose representatives present astute and well prepared speeches which are followed by the rest of the planet acting as a flock of sheep – a flock usually including some black sheep – except when their immediate national interests are directly threatened. We complain, in France, of the "*pensée unique*" (that is this "soft consensus" about the main social aims and the means to realize them). Never have I had a stronger feeling of such a "*pensée unique*" than last year at the General Assembly and I began to get a little nostalgia for the good old days of the Cold War. I had never had great sympathy for the Soviet Empire before it collapsed; but at least, the Cold War made possible a real expression of will by non-western States. All this has disappeared; the "*pensée unique*" prevails, and the delegates from the Third World do not seem to realize that they are manipulated by the West, whose positions are clearly highly ideological ...

This has disastrous effects. Whatever France may think, one of the most positive achievements of the Vienna Convention has certainly been the consolidation of the concept of *jus cogens*, a model of progressive development. Indeed such an achievement would be totally unthinkable today: the intellectual terrorism exercised by the West would categorically exclude this, just as it prepares to kill the notion of crimes, here again one of the most impressive conceptual advances made in the past quarter of the century.

My guess is that, on the occasion of its second reading of the draft on responsibility, the Commission will not dare recant the formidable intuition of Ago which has resulted in the redefinition of the very concept of international responsibility by evacuating damage from its definition.[7] But, while keeping Article 1 (only challenged by a few conservative States, like France or Japan, or scholars, like my master Prosper Weil), the ILC under the adroit guidance of its unfortunately very able new Special Rapporteur on the topic, my friend James Crawford, will abandon Article 19, most of its Members not understanding that, in so doing, first they commit a crime against spirit (the very spirit of the whole of Ago's draft which stands on the assumption that international responsibility is not a pure quasi-contractual matter), and, second, that they are purely and simply endorsing the reactionary fight of a very limited number of industrialized powers which, rightly or not, fear that the legal concept of crime could be used as a legal weapon against their supremacy or leadership.

Well, could you say, and then? Have I not admitted, just a few minutes ago, that one of the main concerns of the ILC should be the acceptability of its drafts? And since States have turned round and, in their majority, seem to have repudiated the notion of crime, why would the ILC maintain it against the whole world? First, very happily, this is not the whole world and there probably exists a majority which, in fact, still endorse the notion of crime; but, with noticeable exceptions, like Italy, for example, if this is a majority, it is a silent majority. In any case, I think that there must be no confusion: acceptability does not mean servility. As legal experts, our role is to explain why a concept is logically and legally necessary and I cannot accept that consistency be sacrificed for reason of a supposed non-acceptability. Yes indeed, we are but the servants of the interests of international

---

[7] On this intellectual "revolution", see Alain Pellet, "Remarques sur une révolution inachevée: le projet d'articles de la CDI sur la responsabilité internationale des États" (1996) AFDI, pp. 7-32. Soon after this paper was delivered, the ILC decided to keep Article 1 of the draft as it had been adopted in first reading; see ILC, Report on the Work of its Fiftieth Session, 20 April-12 June 1998 and 27 July-14 August 1998, UN Doc. GAOR Fifty-Third Session, Supp. N° 10 (A/51/10), paras. 350-354, pp. 151-152. Concerning the notion of crimes, after a very animated debate it has been decided to leave several options open until 1999 (*id.*, paras. 260-321, pp. 123-143).

society and these interests must be defined not by us but by the representatives of States; but, up to now, we have not received any instructions from our political masters to abandon what was, until recently, a widely accepted concept, and which is, it must be repeated again and again, in the line of the whole project and is not for us to presuppose what is the will of States.

As explained above, the most precious aspect of the codification process through the ILC is the constant co-operation of the "expert level" with the "political level"; but, in this process each level must play its own part: the politicians – the States if you prefer – must fix the aims, but they must let us be free to propose; political orientations are their responsibility; conceptual elaboration is our business … And I suggest that we would be well inspired not to invert roles.

This might be easier if States, in nominating and electing Members of the Commission, were more faithful to the letter and, certainly, to the spirit, of our Statute. More and more, they nominate and elect candidates who, in reality, are more acquainted with the United Nations and/or the world of diplomacy than with "academic international law"; this, indeed presents some advantages (it might reinforce support for the Commission and avoids purely metaphysical discussions) but it also has many inconveniences, all the more that, generally speaking, the "professors" come from the West while the "diplomats" are from the Third World. I wish to be understood on this point: I do not suggest that my colleagues are not independent from their Governments; globally they are while they act as ILC Members. What I say is that this creates an imbalance inside the Commission and that its composition erases the *raison d'être* of the whole system, that is the complementarity (the complementarity, not the identification) between the ILC on the one hand and the Sixth Committee on the other hand and, personally, I strongly disapprove the "double cap system", that is the fact that many Members also represent their countries at the Sixth Committee.

Well, all this might not sound very encouraging and you might feel that the ILC is, indeed, definitely not the proper forum to respond to new needs through codification and progressive development, to go back to the sub-title of this presentation. If this is the general feeling, then I have painted too dark a picture. The ILC is far from perfect. It is certainly not ideally composed; it is, nevertheless, made up of (globally) independent lawyers, and the system of regional "quotas", rigid as it may seem, at least guarantees a diversified regional composition and avoids the weaknesses noticeable, for example, in the composition of the Human Rights Committee. Its co-operation with the Sixth Committee is far from ideal; both levels have, nevertheless a constant dialogue. Its process might seem desperately slow; its methods of work have, nevertheless, been improved during the last few years, and they guarantee a serene and in-depth examination of all the facets of a problem; moreover the Commission has shown that, when necessary (or, simply, when it could benefit from the leadership of a dynamic Rapporteur, as Vaclav Mikulka in the case of nationality in relation to the succession of States or James Crawford for the Criminal Court), it can be quick and efficient.

Now, efficient for what? How can the efficiency of a body like the ILC be measured? Expeditiousness? If this is the test, the average is very bad indeed, not far from zero out of twenty (with, once again, bright but very rare exceptions)! But this is not the only criterion. If we take the quality of the output, things rather improve, although I must concede that it is a perfectly subjective judgement.

We could, however, try to make it less subjective by asking the question: what has happened to the ILC drafts? This leads us to statistics. They can be made rather short: up to now the Commission has submitted 26 final reports (if one includes both the Code of Crimes and the Statute of the Criminal Court), plus two first reading drafts (if we include last year's draft on nationality in relation to State succession); these 26 reports have resulted in 15 Conventions (plus a number of optional protocols) but this figure includes the Geneva Conventions of 1958 which were four for the sole topic of the law of the sea and are now *de facto* replaced by the "non-ILC" Montego Bay Convention. Well, let's be generous: 15 Conventions in 50 years ... Not a wonderful achievement apparently ...

I would, however, not be as severe as that: first, several of these treaties, beginning with the Vienna Convention on the Law of Treaties, are among the most important ever concluded; second and above all, it is far from certain that the influence of the work of the ILC can be properly measured through these treaty statistics. As Professor Boyle will cover the topic in the next presentation, I will not enter into any detail concerning the comparative values of "hard treaties" on the one hand and of soft law, of which I am a strong defender, on the other. Suffice it to recall that ILC drafts may exert a considerable influence even before they are completed; just think, in this respect, of the remarkable impact of the Articles on State responsibility and, to take a recent example, of the use the ICJ made of it in its 1997 Judgment in the *Gabc"âkovo/Nagymaros* case[8] ... I also wish to draw your attention to the Introduction to the book published last year by the Commission entitled *International Law on the Eve of the Twenty-First Century* carefully drafted by Members of the Codification Division of the UN, in which "The Achievement of the International Law Commission" is remarkably presented[9].

In view of this and other factors that I have no time to detail, my considered opinion is that the ILC is not an intrinsically bad treaty-maker (or "pre-maker") or, more generally speaking, a bad "codifier"; it is rather

– first, a misused forum; and

– second, one forum among others and not *the* forum, appropriate in all circumstances and for all and every possible topics.

Let me say a word about these *caveats*.

First then, it is a misused forum in the sense that this costly mechanism (it would be worthwhile to calculate the real yearly cost of the ILC . . .) is not provided with topics. This might sound as an odd declaration: don't we have six topics

---

8 *Judgment of 25 September 1997*, 1997 ICJ Rep. p. 7.

9 "Introduction – The Achievement of the International Law Commission", in ILC, *International Law on the Eve of the Twenty-First Century* (United Nations, New York, Sales N° E/F 97.V.4), pp. 1-18.

on our agenda, more than the Commission has ever had? Yes indeed we have six. But only two, inherited from a remote past, have been assigned to the Commission by the General Assembly. The four others are pure "inventions" of the Commission! And I would not dare to explain publicly how one of them at least was selected, but, believe me, it was really in desperation and because we absolutely and urgently needed new topics ... Of course, all these topics have, finally been endorsed by the Sixth Committee, but they have certainly not been chosen by it and, in one case at least, the enthusiasm has been limited, to say the least ...

This being said, with the important exception of "Liability", I think that all these topics are appropriate, and fit for the Commission, as the Commission fits them: they bear on "lawyers' law"; they do not involve too strong short-term political debates; they do not primarily imply expertise in non-legal fields; they do not overlap with similar topics dealt with elsewhere. But the problem remains: do they answer real needs?

My personal answer would be yes, in that, in spite of the lack of enthusiasm of the Sixth Committee for some of them, they give rise to *ex post facto* interest including from non-governmental circles. Indeed, these are not "new needs" in the sense that I presume that most of this distinguished audience, as far as I can understand both from the list of participants and from the titles of the next panels, probably mean by "new needs": more fashionable and "sexy" topics like human rights, disarmament, the law of the environment, or international economic and social law. Well, I would certainly not deny that these too respond to social needs (whether new or not). However, I maintain that the ILC topics too respond, in their own manner, to real needs of the international society.

I would even go so far as to say that they are part of the "constitutional law" of the international society; not in the formal acceptance of the word "constitution" (this would correspond more to the UN Charter or the very rare existing peremptory norms of general international law), but in the substantive sense: they are part of the legal basis in which international society is rooted. This is the case of the law of State responsibility (and of "liability", if only we were able to deal correctly with it!), including diplomatic protection, and of the law of the sources of law as in the case of treaties (through the topic of reservations) or unilateral acts of States. What we do in fact is to consolidate (through progressive development and codification) these legal roots of international society as and when required by its slow process of consolidation.

And, as in all societies, this slowly consolidating international society needs uniform legal rules which transversally cut through all fields covered by international law. I insist: uniform rules. I do not challenge that rules must adapt to their object and that special fields, in some cases, might need special rules. But I strongly regret the new mania in the Commission of advocating "diversity" in all and everything, and in particular, human rights and environment. This way of thinking certainly attracts much sympathy and approval. But I strongly feel that there are limits to this "girondinist" approach – this might be a special joke for the French; let's call it the decentralized or "exploded" approach to international law:

what would one think of a constitution which systematically adopts special rules concerning the adoption or the application of parliamentary acts depending on whether they bear on military or economic or human rights issues? The same holds true concerning treaties: whether human rights activists like it or not, the same general basic rules apply and must apply to all of them. This does not rule out exceptions when exceptions are indispensable, but these exceptions must be included in the *general* codification; and when they are not, they must be provided for in the treaties themselves, not decreed by specialists without paying regard to the need for clear, general, uniform, well established and well respected rules. And this is not that much constraining: after all codified rules are only applicable when the special treaties themselves do not provide otherwise! There is nothing "democratic" or "humanist" in the opposite approach: it only tries to justify the dictatorship of the "specialists" or of the "activists"; it is no more acceptable at the international level than that of the dictatorship of bureaucrats inside the States or in the European Union.

In this respect, I strongly feel that if the ILC did not exist, we should invent it or some kind of similar mechanism. Indeed, one of its main functions is to facilitate and encourage a uniform international law, responding to the needs of international society as a whole. Not its "new needs" maybe; but its constant needs; its "everlasting" needs and its renewed and developing need for uniform transversal rules. This certainly is less exciting, less fashionable, less "sexy" than forging new rules for new needs; but this is a necessary and respectable task which could, certainly, be performed in a better and more efficient way. But, for the time being, let the ILC live … *faute de mieux*! and for the "new needs", let other forums, better equipped for that, and unavoidably more political, deal with them. This is, for me, a perfectly acceptable sharing of the tasks.

ALAN BOYLE*

Some Reflections on the Relationship of Treaties and Soft Law

INTRODUCTION

My starting point for this discussion of the relationship between treaties and soft law is the observation that the subtlety of the processes by which contemporary international law can be created is no longer adequately captured by reference to the orthodox categories of custom and treaty. The role of soft law as an element in international law-making is now widely appreciated, and its influence throughout international law is evident. Within that law-making process the relationships between treaty and custom, or between soft law and custom, are also well understood. The relationship between treaties and soft law is less often explored, but it is no less important, and has great practical relevance to the work of international organizations.

WHAT IS SOFT LAW?

Soft law has a wide range of possible meanings,[1] but three are of direct relevance to the present enquiry:

Soft Law is Not Binding

When used in this sense soft law can be contrasted with hard law, which is binding. Treaties are by definition always hard law because they are always binding. In this category of soft law the legal form is decisive: if the form is that of a treaty it can-

* This chapter is reproduced from (1999) 48 ICLQ, p. 901.

1 See generally R. R. Baxter, "International Law in 'Her Infinite Variety'" (1980) 29 ICLQ, pp. 549-566; C. M. Chinkin, "The Challenge of Soft Law: Development and Change in International Law" (1989) 38 ICLQ, pp. 850-866; Pierre-Marie Dupuy, "Soft Law and the International Law of the Environment" (1991) 12 Michigan JIL, pp. 420-435; Jerzy Sztucki, "Reflections on International Soft Law", in (1992) *de Lege*, p. 365.

V. Gowlland-Debbas (ed.), Multilateral Treaty-making, 25–38.

not be soft law. If the form is that of a non-binding agreement, such as the Helsinki Accords,[2] it will not be a treaty for precisely that reason and we will have what is in effect a "soft" agreement. Of course, the question whether an agreement is a binding treaty is not necessarily easy to answer, as we can observe in the *Qatar-Bahrain Maritime Delimitation Case*.[3] Moreover, an agreement involving States may be binding even if it is not a treaty,[4] so the distinction between hard and soft agreements is not simply synonymous with the distinction between treaties and non-treaties. Moreover, once soft law begins to interact with binding treaties its non-binding character may be lost or altered.

Soft Law Consists of General Norms or Principles, Not Rules

An alternative view of soft law focuses on the contrast between "rules", involving clear and reasonably specific commitments which are in this sense hard law, and "norms" or "principles", which, being more open-textured or general in their content and wording, can thus be seen as soft. From this perspective treaties may be either hard or soft, or both, as we shall see later in regard to the Convention on Climate Change. In this category it is the content of the treaty provision which is decisive in determining whether it is hard or soft, not its form as a treaty.

Soft Law is Law that is Not Readily Enforceable through Binding Dispute Resolution

Here the contrast is between a treaty subject to compulsory adjudication in cases of dispute, such as the 1982 UN Convention on the Law of the Sea,[5] and a treaty or other instrument under which disputes can be referred unilaterally only to non-binding conciliation or a non-binding compliance procedure, such as the Montreal Protocol to the Convention on the Ozone Layer.[6] These examples represent only some of the gradations on a spectrum of possibilities, which shade ultimately into dispute avoidance, but in this category it is the character of the dispute resolution process which determines whether we have hard or soft law.

What is obvious from this discussion is that the distinction between treaty and soft law is not clear cut: a treaty can be both hard and soft, and in several different senses at once. Of itself this is neither contradictory nor problematic, so long as we are clear about what we mean when we use the terms hard and soft law. Bearing this caveat in mind, we can now explore the relationship between treaties and soft law more fully.

---

2 Oscar Schachter, "The Twilight Existence of Non-Binding International Agreements" (1977) 71 AJIL, pp. 296-304.

3 *Maritime Delimitation and Territorial Questions between Qatar and Bahrain (Jurisdiction and Admissibility)* (1994) ICJ Rep. 112.

4 For example an agreement between a State and a multinational company: see *Anglo-Iranian Oil Co. (Jurisdiction)* (1952) ICJ Rep. 93.

5 *Infra*, n. 36.

6 *Infra*, n. 40.

SOFT-LAW AS NON-BINDING LAW

Reliance on soft law as part of the law-making process takes a number of different forms, including declarations of intergovernmental conferences, such as the Rio Declaration on Environment and Development; resolutions of the UN General Assembly, such as those dealing with outer space, the deep seabed, decolonization, or permanent sovereignty over natural resources; or codes of conduct, guidelines and recommendations of international organizations, such as IAEA, IMO, UNEP or FAO. While the legal effect of these different soft law instruments is not necessarily the same, it is characteristic of all of them that they are carefully negotiated, and often carefully drafted statements, which are in some cases intended to have some normative significance despite their non-binding, non-treaty form. There is at least an element of good faith commitment, and in many cases, a desire to influence State practice and an element of law-making intention and progressive development. In this sense non-binding soft law instruments are not fundamentally different from those multilateral treaties which serve much the same law-making purposes. In this respect they may be both an alternative to and a part of the process of multilateral treaty-making.

Soft Law as an Alternative to Law-Making by Treaty

There are several reasons why soft law instruments may represent an attractive alternative to law-making by treaty. First, it may be easier to reach agreement when the form is non-binding. Use of soft law instruments enables States to agree to more detailed and precise provisions because their legal commitment, and the consequences of any non-compliance, are more limited. Secondly, it may be easier for some States to adhere to non-binding instruments because they can avoid the domestic treaty ratification process, and perhaps escape democratic accountability for the policy to which they have agreed. Of course this may also make it comparably harder to implement such policies if funding, legislation, or public support are necessary. Thirdly, soft law instruments will normally be easier to amend or replace than treaties, particularly when all that is required is the adoption of a new resolution by an international institution. Treaties take time to replace or amend, and the attempt to do so can result in an awkward and overlapping network of old and new obligations between different sets of parties. One of the better examples of the confused state of the law which can result is the 1929 Warsaw Convention Relating to International Carriage by Air.[7] Lastly, soft law instruments may provide more immediate evidence of international support and consensus than a treaty whose impact is heavily qualified by reservations and the need to wait for ratification and entry into force.

Given the relative advantages of soft law over treaties, it is perhaps surprising that the multilateral treaty has until now been the International Law Commission's

---

[7] See Richard Gardiner, "Revising the Law of Carriage by Air: Mechanisms in Treaties and Contract" (1998) 47 ICLQ, pp. 278-305.

preferred instrument for the codification of international law.[8] Although a treaty basis may be required when creating new international organizations or institutions, or for dispute settlement provisions, soft law instruments appear to be just as useful a means of codifying international law as treaties. Provided they contain no binding dispute settlement clauses, the Commission's draft articles on the law of State responsibility could equally well be codified using either a General Assembly resolution or an intergovernmental declaration.[9] Indeed this may be more effective than using a treaty, which, like the Vienna Convention on the Law of Treaties, runs the risk of securing only a relatively small number of parties. The Commission's work on treaties is among its most successful and authoritative codifications, but it is difficult to suggest that this owes much to its treaty status, or to the number of States parties.

The argument for using a treaty rather than a soft law instrument is stronger in the case of new law-making, such as the re-negotiation of the law of the sea or the elaboration of human rights law, although in many of these cases institutions with extensive powers were also being established at the same time and a treaty was thus desirable in any event. But even for new law, non-binding instruments may still be useful if they can help generate widespread and consistent State practice and/or provide evidence of *opinio juris* in support of a customary rule. There are good examples of UN General Assembly resolutions and intergovernmental declarations having this effect in the *Nicaragua Case,*[10] the *Nuclear Weapons Advisory Opinion,*[11] and the *Gabčíkovo -Nagymaros Project Case.*[12]

What all of this suggests is that the non-binding form of an instrument is of relatively limited relevance in the context of customary international law-making. Treaties do not generate or codify customary law because of their binding form but because they either influence State practice and provide evidence of opinio juris for new or emerging rules, or because they are good evidence of what the existing law is. In many cases this is no different from the potential effect of non-binding soft law instruments. Both treaties and soft law instruments can be vehicles for focusing consensus on rules and principles, and for mobilising a consistent, general response on the part of States. Depending upon what is involved, treaties may be more effective than soft law instruments for this purpose because they indicate a stronger commitment to the principles in question and to that extent carry greater weight than a soft law instrument, but the assumption that they are necessarily

---

8 Articles 17 and 23 of the Statute of the Commission do refer expressly to the conclusion of conventions, but other possibilities are left open.

9 The Commission considered the eventual form of its draft articles at its 50th Session in 1998 but deferred a decision on whether to propose a convention or a declaration. It was noted that the dispute settlement provisions in part three of the draft could not be included in a declaration.

10 (1986) ICJ Rep. 14.

11 (1996) ICJ Rep. 226.

12 (1997) ICJ Rep. 7.

more authoritative is misplaced. To take only one example, it is clear that the 1992 Rio Declaration on Environment and Development both codifies some existing international law and tries to develop some new law.[13] It is not obvious that a treaty with the same provisions would carry greater weight or achieve its objectives any more successfully. On the contrary, it is quite possible that such a treaty would, seven years later, still have far from universal participation, whereas the Declaration secured immediate consensus support, with such authority as that implies. At the same time, it seems clear that agreements such as those on climate change and biological diversity could only be in treaty form, because of the combination of their status as new law, their more detailed terms, and their institutional provisions. These are good examples of cases where because of the content of an agreement, incorporation in a treaty is the right option and does carry a greater sense of commitment than a soft law instrument.

Soft Law as Part of the Multilateral Treaty-Making Process

Some non-binding soft-law instruments are significant only because they are the first step in a process eventually leading to conclusion of a multilateral treaty. Examples are numerous, but they include the IAEA Guidelines[14] which formed the basis for the rapid adoption of the 1986 Convention on Early Notification of a Nuclear Accident following the Chernobyl accident; UNEP Guidelines on Environmental Impact Assessment[15] which were subsequently substantially incorporated in the 1991 ECE Convention on Environmental Impact Assessment in a Transboundary Context; and UNEP's Guidelines on Land-based Sources of Marine Pollution,[16] which provided a model for regional treaties such as the Kuwait Protocol.[17]

Other soft law instruments are used as mechanisms for authoritative interpretation or amplification of the terms of a treaty. This has occasionally been the role of General Assembly resolutions in regard to articles of the UN Charter, such as those dealing with decolonization or the use of force.[18] The same task is performed more frequently by resolutions, recommendations and decisions of other international organizations, and by the conferences of parties to treaties. Thus it was a resolution of the parties to the Montreal Protocol to the Ozone Convention which first set out the terms of the non-compliance procedure provided for in the proto-

---

13 See Alan Boyle and David Freestone (eds.), *International Law and Sustainable Development: Past Achievements and Future Prospects* (Oxford University Press, Oxford, 1999), ch.1; Philippe Sands (ed.), *Greening International Law* (Earthscan, London, 1993), chs. 1 and 3.

14 IAEA/INFCIRC/321 (1985).

15 UNEP/GC14/25 (1987).

16 UNEP/WG.120/3 (1985).

17 1990 Kuwait Protocol for the Protection of the Marine Environment Against Marine Pollution from Land-based Sources.

18 See *Western Sahara (Advisory Opinion)* (1975) ICJ Rep. 12; *Military and Paramilitary Activities in and against Nicaragua* (*Nicaragua v. United States of America*) (*Merits)* (1986) ICJ Rep. 14.

col.[19] The procedure was subsequently revised and then incorporated by amendment as an annex in the protocol,[20] showing again how non-binding soft law can often be readily transformed into binding form. Similarly, UNEP's Cairo Guidelines on the Transport of Hazardous Wastes[21] can be regarded as an amplification of the obligation of "environmentally sound management" provided for in the Basel Convention on the Control of Transboundary Movements of Hazardous Wastes.[22]

Another important related role for soft law instruments is to provide the detailed rules and technical standards required for implementation of some treaties. Environmental soft law is quite often important for this reason, setting standards of best practice or due diligence to be achieved by the parties in implementing their obligations. These "ecostandards" are essential in giving hard content to the overly-general and open-textured terms of framework environmental treaties.[23] The advantages of regulating environmental risks in this way are that the detailed rules can easily be changed or strengthened as scientific understanding develops or as political priorities change. Such standards can of course be adopted in binding form, using easily amended annexes to provide flexibility, but this is not always what parties want. The IAEA has made particular use of formally non-binding ecostandards, through its nuclear safety codes and principles. These generally represent an authoritative technical and political consensus, approved by the Board of Governors or General Conference of the Agency. Despite their soft law status it is relatively easy to see them as minimum internationally endorsed standards of conduct, and to regard failure to comply as presumptively a failure to fulfil the customary obligation of due diligence in the regulation and control of nuclear activities.[24] However, because of the uncertainty posed by this very soft approach to nuclear safety, the Convention on Nuclear Safety and the Joint Convention on the Safety of Spent Fuel and Radioactive Waste Management have now incorporated in binding treaty articles the main elements of IAEA's fundamental safety standards for nuclear installations, radioactive waste management and radiation protection, and most of its Code of Practice on the Transboundary Movement of Radioactive Waste.[25] Those remaining IAEA standards which retain a soft law

---

19 Decision II/5, UNEP/OzL.Pro/WG.3/2/2, Annex III (1990).

20 *Infra*, note 40.

21 UNEP/WG.122/3.

22 Article 4.

23 See Paolo Contini and Peter H. Sand, "Methods to Expedite Environment Protection: International Ecostandards" (1972) 66 AJIL, pp. 37-59.

24 The preamble to the Nuclear Safety Convention recognises that internationally formulated safety guidelines "can provide guidance on contemporary means of achieving a high level of safety." IAEA guidelines would be the obvious starting point for determining what constituted the "appropriate steps" with regard to safety controls required by Articles 10-19 of the Convention.

25 IAEA Safety Series No.110: *The Safety of Nuclear Installations* (Vienna, 1993); IAEA Safety Series No.111-F: *The Principles of Radioactive Waste Management* (Vienna,

status[26] will still be relevant when determining how the basic obligations of States parties to these agreements are to be implemented. Moreover, under the Joint Convention there is also an obligation on States parties to take account of relevant IAEA standards in adopting national law. These various agreements have significantly strengthened the legal force of IAEA standards and, in conjunction with non-binding soft-law safety standards, have created a more convincing legal framework for the international regulation of nuclear risks. They exemplify once again how soft-law and treaties can interact in a complex regulatory framework.

Some treaties give binding force to soft-law instruments by incorporating them into the terms of a treaty by implied reference. The 1982 UN Convention on the Law of the Sea makes extensive use of this technique, impliedly incorporating recommendations and resolutions of IMO, as well as treaties such as the 1973 MARPOL Convention, under provisions variously requiring or permitting States to apply "generally accepted rules and standards established through the competent international organization or general diplomatic conference".[27] Thus although IMO has no power under its constitution to take formally binding decisions, UNCLOS may indirectly render some of these decisions obligatory.

Lastly, soft law instruments may operate in conjunction with a treaty to provide evidence of *opinio juris* for the possible emergence of a rule of customary international law. ICJ case law, including the *Nicaragua Case*, shows how the interplay between the UN Charter and resolutions of the General Assembly can have this effect.

These examples all point to the conclusion that the non-binding force of soft-law can be over-stated. In many of the above examples States are not necessarily free to disregard applicable soft-law instruments: even when not incorporated directly into a treaty, they may represent an agreed understanding of its terms. Thus, although of themselves these instruments may not be legally binding, their interaction with related treaties may transform their legal status into something more.

SOFT LAW AS GENERAL NORMS OR PRINCIPLES

The point was made many years ago by the late Judge Baxter that some treaties are soft in the sense that they impose no real obligations on the parties.[28] Though formally binding, the vagueness, indeterminacy, or generality of their provisions may deprive them of the character of "hard law" in any meaningful sense. This remains true. The Framework Convention on Climate Change provides a good example.

1995); IAEA Safety Series No.120: *Radiation Protection and the Safety of Radiation Sources* (Vienna, 1996); IAEA GC (XXXIV)/939: *Code of Practice on the Transboundary Movement of Nuclear Waste* (1990).

26 E.g. the NUSS codes, IAEA GC (XXXII)/489 (1988).

27 1982 UN Convention on the Law of the Sea, Articles 207-212.

28 (1980) 29 ICLQ, pp. 549-566.

Adopted at the Rio Conference in 1992; this treaty does impose some commitments on the parties, but its core articles, dealing with policies and measures to tackle greenhouse gas emissions, are so cautiously and obscurely worded and so weak that it is uncertain whether any real obligations are created.[29] Moreover, whatever commitments have been undertaken by developing States are also conditional on performance of solidarity commitments by developed State parties to provide funding and transfer of technology.[30] Such treaty provisions are almost impossible to breach and in that limited sense Judge Baxter is justified in calling them soft law. More of a political bargain than a legal one, these are "soft" undertakings of a very fragile kind. They are not normative and cannot be described as creating "rules" in any meaningful sense. This is probably true of very many, if not most treaties, a point recognized by the International Court in the *North Sea Continental Shelf Case* when it specified that one of the conditions to be met before a treaty could be regarded as law-making is that it should be so drafted as to be "potentially normative" in character.[31]

There is, however, a second and more significant sense in which a treaty may be potentially normative, but still "soft" in character, because it articulates "principles" rather than "rules". Such principles do have legal significance in much the same way that Dworkin uses the idea of constitutional principles.[32] They may lay down parameters which affect the way courts decide cases,[33] or the way an international institution exercises its discretionary powers. They can set limits, or provide guidance, or determine how conflicts between other rules or principles will be resolved. They may lack the supposedly harder edge of a "rule" or an "obligation", but they are certainly not legally irrelevant. As such they constitute a very important form of law, which may be "soft", but which should not be confused with "non-binding" law.

The Convention on Climate Change once again provides some good examples of such principles explicitly included in a major treaty. Indeed, given how weak the rest of the treaty is, the principles found in Article 3 are arguably the most impor-

---

29 Especially Articles 4(1) and (2). The United States' interpretation of these articles was that "there is nothing in any of the language which constitutes a commitment to any specific level of emissions at any time..." The parties determined at their first meeting in 1995 that the commitments were inadequate and they agreed to commence negotiation of the much more specific commitments now contained in the 1997 Kyoto Protocol.

30 Article 4(7).

31 *North Sea Continental Shelf (Judgement)* (1969) ICJ Rep. 3.

32 Ronald Dworkin, *Taking Rights Seriously* (Duckworth, London, 1977). This argument is developed by Philippe Sands, in, Winfried Lang (ed.), *Sustainable Development and International Law* (Graham & Trotman/Martinus Nijhoff, London/Dordrecht/Boston, 1995), ch.5.

33 E.g. the International Court's reliance on the principle of sustainable development in the *Gabčíkovo -Nagymaros Case*, on which see Vaughan Lowe, in Boyle and Freestone, *International Law and Sustainable Development, op. cit.*, ch. 2, and A. E. Boyle, "The *Gabčíkovo -Nagymaros* Case: New Law in Old Bottles" (1997) 8 *Yearbook of International Environmental Law* 13-20.

tant "law" in the whole agreement because they prescribe how the regime for regulating climate change is to be developed by the parties. It is worth quoting the main elements of Article 3:

Article 3: Principles

In their actions to achieve the objective of the Convention and to implement its provisions, the parties shall be guided, *inter alia*, by the following:

1. The Parties should protect the climate system for the benefit of present and future generations of humankind, on the basis of equity and in accordance with their common but differentiated responsibilities …
3. The Parties should take precautionary measures to anticipate, prevent, or minimise the causes of climate change and mitigate its adverse effects …
4. The Parties have a right to, and should, promote sustainable development …

These elements of Article 3 are all drawn directly from the non-binding Rio Declaration on Environment and Development; they reflect principles which are not simply part of the Climate Change Convention, but which are also emerging at the level of general international law, even if it is as yet premature to accord them the status of customary international law. They are not expressed in obligatory terms: the use of "should" qualifies their application, despite the obligatory wording of the chapeau sentence. All of these principles are open-textured in the sense that there is considerable uncertainty concerning their specific content and they leave much room for interpretation and elaboration. They are not at all like rules requiring States to conduct an environmental impact assessment, or to prevent harm to other States.

Given their explicit role as guidance and their explicitly softer formulation, the "principles" in Article 3 are not necessarily binding rules which must be complied with or which entail responsibility for breach if not complied with; yet, despite all these limitations they are not legally irrelevant.[34] At the very least Article 3 is relevant to interpretation and implementation of the Convention as well as creating expectations concerning matters which must be taken into account in good faith in the negotiation of further instruments.

Article 3 takes a novel approach to environmental protection, but in the context of a dynamic and evolutionary regulatory regime such as the Climate Change Convention it has the important merit of providing some predictability regarding the parameters within which the parties are required to work towards the objective of the Convention. In particular, they are not faced with a completely blank sheet of paper when entering subsequent protocol negotiations or when the Conference of the Parties takes decisions under the various articles empowering it to do so. Thus it is significant that the relevance of Article 3 was reiterated in the mandate for

---

[34] See the debate between Philippe Sands and Howard Mann (Ph. Sands, "International Law in the Field of Sustainable Development: Emerging Legal Principles" and Howard Mann, "Comment on the Paper by P.S." in Lang, *Sustainable Development, op. cit.*, 53-74 at 53-66 and 67-72, respectively).

negotiation of the Kyoto Protocol[35] and is referred to in the preamble to the Protocol. It is a nice question whether the parties collectively are entitled to disregard the principles contained in Article 3, or what the legal effect of decisions which do so may be, but however weak it may seem, parties whose interests are affected do have a right to insist on having the principles of Article 3 taken into account. Sustainable development, intergenerational equity, or the precautionary principle, are all more convincingly seen in this sense: not as binding obligations which must be complied with, but as principles, considerations or objectives to be taken account of – they may be soft, but they are still law.

Soft Enforcement

Another way of distinguishing hard and soft law is to focus not on questions of form or content but on methods of dispute settlement in case of non-compliance. What might be called hard enforcement is characterised most obviously by compulsory binding settlement of disputes. The 1982 UN Convention on the Law of the Sea is one of the foremost examples of a treaty which is subject to hard enforcement through a sophisticated scheme of compulsory dispute settlement involving both the ICJ and the International Tribunal for the Law of the Sea, as well as various forms of arbitration.[36] The Convention also affirms that States are responsible in international law for the performance of their environmental obligations under the Convention,[37] and in various circumstances it gives them either the power or the duty to use their own criminal law to enforce internationally agreed rules and standards against ships.[38] All of these elements add up to a treaty which is hard in every sense of the term.

The contrasting model of "soft enforcement", or "dispute avoidance", is one in which problems are referred to non-binding conciliation before an independent

---

35 The so-called "Berlin mandate": Decision 1/CP.1, in, *Report of the Conference of the Parties on its 1st Session,* UN Doc.FCCC/CP/1995/7/Add.1.

36 See Part XV, on which see Alan Boyle, "Dispute Settlement and the Law of the Sea Convention: Problems of Fragmentation and Jurisdiction", (1997) 46 ICLQ, pp. 37-54; Robin Churchill, "Dispute Settlement in the Law of the Sea – The Context of the International Tribunal for the Law of the Sea and Alternatives to it", in Malcolm Evans (ed.), *Remedies in International Law: The Institutional Dilemma* (Hart Pub., Oxford, 1998), pp. 85-109; John Merrills, *International Dispute Settlement* (3rd ed., Grotius, Cambridge, 1999), ch. 8; R. R. Churchill and A.V. Lowe, *The Law of the Sea* (3rd ed., Manchester University Press, Manchester, 1999), ch. 19; L. B. Sohn, "Settlement of Law of the Sea Disputes" (1995) 10 *Int. J. of Marine and Coastal Law,* pp. 205-217; Andronico Adede, *The System for Settlement of Disputes Under the United Nations Convention on the Law of the Sea: a Drafting History and a Commentary* (Martinus Nijhoff, Dordrecht/Boston, 1987); E. D. Brown, "Dispute Settlement and the Law of the Sea: the UN Convention Regime" (1997) 21 *Marine Policy,* pp. 17-43.

37 Article 235(1).

38 Articles 216-218, 220.

third party, or to some form of non-compliance procedure involving other parties to the treaty.[39] In both situations there is an attempt to find an agreed solution, rather than to engage in adversarial litigation or claims for reparation. Soft enforcement characteristically evades issues of responsibility for breach, and relies on a combination of inducements or the possibility of termination or suspension of treaty rights to secure compliance.

Soft enforcement is best exemplified by the non-compliance procedure adopted by parties to the 1987 Montreal Protocol to the Ozone Convention.[40] This procedure, adopted in 1990 and revised in 1992, can be invoked by any party to the protocol, or by the protocol secretariat, or by the party itself, wherever there are thought to be problems regarding compliance. The matter is then referred for investigation to an Implementation Committee consisting of 10 parties elected on the basis of equitable geographical representation. The main task of this committee is to consider the submissions, information and observations made to it with a view to securing an amicable solution of the matter on the basis of respect for the provisions of the Protocol. This is very similar to the provision for negotiation of a friendly settlement under the European Convention on Human Rights.[41] The Implementation Committee can seek whatever information it needs through the secretariat; for this purpose it may also visit the territory of the party under investigation if invited to do so. A report is then made to the full Meeting of the Parties, which decides what steps to call for in order to bring about full compliance. These can include the provision of appropriate financial, technical, or training assistance in order to help the party to comply. If these measures are insufficient, cautions can be issued, or, as a last resort, rights and privileges under the treaty can be suspended in accordance with the law of treaties. A very similar

---

[39] See Andronico Adede, in Lang, *Sustainable Development, op. cit.*, ch. 8; Patricia W. Birnie, "Legal Techniques of Settling Disputes: The 'Soft Settlement' Approach", in William E. Butler (ed.), *Perestroika and International Law* (Martinus Nijhoff, Dordrecht/Boston, 1990), pp. 177-195; Thomas Gehring, "International Environmental Regimes: Dynamic Sectoral Legal Systems" (1990) 1 *Yearbook of International Environmental Law*, pp. 35-56; Günther Handl, "Controlling Implementation of and Compliance with International Environmental Commitments: The Rocky Road From Rio" (1994) 5 Colorado JIELP, pp. 305-331; Alexandre-Charles Kiss, "Compliance with International and European Environmental Obligations" (1996) 9 *Hague Yearbook of International Law*, pp. 45-54; Winfried Lang, "Compliance Control in International Environmental Law: Institutional Necessities" (1996) 56 ZaöRV, pp. 685-695.

[40] Article 8, and Annex IV, as adopted at Copenhagen in 1992. The process is described in UNEP, *Report of the Implementation Committee for the Montreal Protocol, 20th Meeting*, UNEP/OzL.Pro/ImpCom/20/4, paras. 24-33; O. Yoshida, "Soft Enforcement of Treaties: The Montreal Non-compliance Procedure and the Functions of Internal International Institutions" (1999) 10 Colorado JIELP, pp. 95-141.

[41] Protocol 11 of the European Convention on Human Rights; Article 38 provides that the Court of Human Rights "shall place itself at the disposal of the parties concerned with a view to securing a friendly settlement of the matter on the basis of respect for human rights as defined in the Convention" and the Protocols thereto.

procedure has been adopted under the 1979 Convention on Long Range Transboundary Air Pollution.[42]

The non-compliance procedure has been invoked on several occasions by parties to the Montreal Protocol who are in difficulty, notably Russia and a number of other States from the former Soviet Union, where problems of non-compliance have been the most serious. Various measures have been recommended by the Meeting of the Parties, including the provision of assistance, GEF funding, and the issuing of cautions.[43] Further funding from the GEF has also been conditional on the Meeting of the Parties certifying that progress is satisfactory. The effect has been to secure compliance, albeit at the cost of some delay in implementation.

There is also provision in Article 18 of the Kyoto Protocol to the Framework Convention on Climate Change for a non-compliance procedure to be negotiated. Developing a process capable of handling the more complex commitments undertaken for climate change is not straightforward and none had yet been agreed at the time of writing.[44] However, the Climate Change Convention has created another innovation in "soft settlement" through the provision for a "multilateral consultative process" to resolve questions regarding implementation.[45] This process can be extended to the Kyoto Protocol if the parties so decide. It is intended to be an even softer form of dispute avoidance than the Montreal Protocol non-compliance procedure: conducted by a panel of experts, rather than by other member States, it is non-judicial in character, non-confrontational, and advisory rather than supervisory. No sanctions of any kind can be imposed, not even suspension of rights and privileges; there is power only to recommend measures to facilitate co-operation and implementation and to clarify issues and promote understanding of the Con-

---

42 See Decision 1997/2, in, UNECE, *Report of the 15th Session of the Executive Body* (1997), Annex III and Patrick Széll, "The Development of Multilateral Mechanisms for Monitoring Compliance", in Lang, *Sustainable Development, op. cit.*, pp. 97-109.

43 See UNEP, *Report of the 7th Meeting of the Parties to the Montreal Protocol*, Decisions VII/15-19 (Poland, Bulgaria, Belarus, Russia, Ukraine) UNEP/OzL.Pro.7/12 (1995); *id.*, *Report of the 8th Meeting*, Decisions VIII/22-25 (Latvia, Lithuania, Czech Republic, Russia) UNEP/OzL.Pro.8/12 (1996); *id.*, *Report of the 9th Meeting*, Decisions IX/29-32 (Latvia, Lithuania, Russia, Czech Republic) UNEP/OzL.Pro.9/12 (1997). For the most recent position see *Report of the Implementation Committee for the Montreal Protocol*, *20th Meeting*, UNEP/OzL.Pro/ImpCom/20/4 (1998). See generally Jacob Werksman, "Compliance and Transition: Russia's Non-Compliance Tests the Ozone Regime" (1996) 36 ZaöRV p. 750; David G. Victor, *The Early Operation and Effectiveness of the Montreal Protocol's Non-compliance Procedure* (International Institute for Applied Systems Analysis, Laxenburg, 1996); Richard E. Benedick, *Ozone Diplomacy: New Directions in Safeguarding the Planet* (Enlarged ed., Harvard University Press, Cambridge, Mass., 1998), ch.17.

44 The problems are discussed in Jacob Werksman, *Responding to Non-Compliance Under the Climate Change Regime* (OECD, 1998); *id.* in James Cameron, Jacob Werksman, Peter Roderick (eds.), *Improving Compliance with International Environmental Law*, (Earthscan, 1996), pp. 85 *et seq.*

45 1992 UNFCCC Article 13; 1997 Kyoto Protocol Article 16. For details of the process see *6th Report of the Ad Hoc Working Group on Article 13* (1998) UN Doc. FCCC/AG13/1998/2.

vention. As in the Montreal Protocol non-compliance procedure, parties may bring questions concerning their own implementation or that of other parties to the Multilateral Consultative Committee; the Conference of the Parties may also do so.

This new process represents a further move away from formal, binding, third party dispute settlement in favour of procedures that facilitate compliance but cannot compel it. Like the Montreal Protocol procedure it tries to resolve problems, differences, or disputes, through political rather than judicial processes, relying on negotiation and persuasion, rather than formal findings of breach of treaty or responsibility. "Soft enforcement" of this kind is not confined to environmental agreements; it has however been criticised by Koskenniemi for undermining the binding character of the treaties concerned and setting them apart from "normal" treaties.[46] It does give us, as we have seen, another category of "soft" treaty. Why do States employ these techniques of soft enforcement for certain treaties? There are several reasons.

First, like non-binding instruments, it facilitates agreement on rules or commitments which are hard in content. These rules or commitments do have the binding force of a treaty, with all that implies in terms of a sense of obligation, but the consequences of non-compliance are not as severe or potentially troublesome as they would be if there were compulsory binding adjudication in every case of dispute or alleged non-compliance. This may be important in areas such as climate change, where compliance is not equally easy for all States, or where the capacities of States differ. It allows some leeway for parties in difficulty, while the emphasis on co-operation is consistent with broader notions of solidarity which underlie many modern environmental agreements. Secondly, soft enforcement is more suited to a regulatory approach which emphasises prevention of problems rather than reparation after the event. Thirdly, where, as in the case of climate change or ozone depletion, non-compliance affects all parties to the treaty equally, there is considerable merit in designing a process for securing compliance which is multilateral in character and which allows all parties, as well as NGOs, to participate, and which ensures that all interests are adequately represented. Although it is possible to accommodate a multiplicity of parties and NGOs in judicial proceedings,[47] it is not easy to do so, and an adversarial procedure is not well suited to the resolution of the kind of non-compliance problems likely to arise under global environmental treaties. Lastly, soft enforcement typically facilitates more readily than judicial processes the necessary input of scientific and technical expertise required

---

[46] Martti Koskenniemi, "Breach of Treaty or Non-Compliance? Reflections on the Enforcement of the Montreal Protocol" (1992) 3 *Yearbook of International Environmental Law*, pp. 123-162.

[47] See for example the *Nuclear Weapons (Advisory Opinion)*, (1996) ICJ Rep. 226, in which some 40 States made written or oral submissions to the Court. In contentious cases involving the construction of a multilateral convention all parties to the convention have a right to intervene in the proceedings, and the construction so given will be equally binding on such States: Statute of the ICJ, Article 66. It should be noted, however, that an allegation of non-compliance is not necessarily a question of construction.

to deal with issues of compliance under agreements of this kind. That is probably the major contribution of the processes of review developed under the Ozone and Climate Change Conventions.

None of this is to deny that hard settlement should remain an option under any of these treaties, in case the parties to a dispute should choose to resort to it. The evidence referred to earlier suggests that Koskenniemi's scepticism may be misplaced with regard to the operation of the Montreal Protocol's non-compliance procedure. Whether the same judgment can in due course be made in relation to the much more difficult and complex problem of climate change remains to be seen. It is of course wise to avoid disputes regarding compliance with treaties, or with softer instruments, but it is also necessary to have some assurance that they can be resolved, if not by persuasion and negotiation, then by some other authoritative process. From that perspective hard and soft enforcement are perhaps better seen not as alternatives but as complementary to each other.

CONCLUSIONS

Soft law is manifestly a multi-faceted concept, whose relationship to treaties is both subtle and diverse. It presents alternatives to treaties in certain circumstances, at other times it complements them, while also providing different ways of understanding the legal effect of different kinds of treaty. Those who maintain that soft law is simply not law have perhaps missed some of the points made here; moreover those who see a treaty as necessarily having greater legal effect than soft law have perhaps not looked hard enough at the "infinite variety" of treaties, to quote Baxter once more. Soft law in its various forms can of course be abused, but so can most legal forms, and it has generally been more helpful to the process of international law-making than it has been objectionable. It is simply another tool in the professional lawyer's armoury.

Participation in Multilateral Treaty-Making by Non-State Entities

Chair: ANDREW CLAPHAM

LOUISE DOSWALD-BECK

Participation of Non-Governmental Entities in Treaty-Making: the Case of Conventional Weapons

GROWING IMPORTANCE OF CIVIL SOCIETY

Civil society has become an important participant in today's multilateral treaty-making, thanks in large part to the considerable significance States now accord its work. This is particularly true in the field of international humanitarian law, where the interest of civil society has traditionally been represented by the International Committee of the Red Cross (ICRC) – an organization that, according to its Statutes adopted by States, works towards the creation of international humanitarian treaties. In recent years, non-governmental organizations (NGOs) likewise have come to perform similar tasks.

Broadly speaking, there are two main stages of participation by non-governmental entities, the ICRC and NGOs alike, in multilateral treaty-making: the pre-diplomatic conference stage and the diplomatic conference stage. Non-governmental entities exert their influence not only in situations where their advocacy *culminates* in a diplomatic conference – as was clearly the case in the Ottawa process on anti-personal landmines – but also where such a conference is already foreseen, for example in order to conduct a periodic review, update and/or amend an existing instrument, such as Protocol II of the 1980 Convention on Certain Conventional Weapons (CCW).

BEFORE THE DIPLOMATIC CONFERENCE

Prior to a diplomatic conference, non-governmental entities impact the treaty-making process through various means. Their most important work during this pre-diplomatic conference stage is fact-finding.

It is imperative that such fact-finding meet the highest standard of accuracy. Indeed, the experiences of the late-1970s for the 1980 CCW Convention show that an initiative based on inaccurate or incomplete information will never successfully dispel objections and suspicions raised by States. Credibility should be achieved

V. Gowlland-Debbas (ed.), Multilateral Treaty-making, 41–44.

through research, consultation with experts and publication of reports on the subject. The ICRC, for example, undertook these activities within the context of conventional weapons for the review conference of the 1980 CCW Convention, and more specifically, convened several expert meetings during the campaign for a total ban on anti-personal landmines.

Credible fact-finding is likewise an invaluable tool for the creation of interest among States on an issue. Through bilateral contacts or governmental expert meetings, humanitarian advocates use reliable information to sensitize States, persuading them that a specific concern – the harmful effects of anti-personal landmines, for instance – is indeed an urgent issue which requires the attention of the international community. Conversely, unreliable information will be unpersuasive; a State that questions the accuracy of information furnished by non-governmental entities is likely to remain unmoved, unconvinced of the cause itself.

Creating State interest in an issue often involves further action, such as co-operation with other members of civil society. For example, as a neutral international organization, the ICRC is not well placed to involve itself too deeply within a State. In the case of blinding laser weapons, therefore, the ICRC was fortunate to receive support from Human Rights Watch, an influential U.S.-based NGO able to speak with its own government and operate effectively within that country.

Co-operation between members of civil society on a specific issue may take the form of a coalition. This is particularly beneficial for large numbers of NGOs working independently on the same concern; a coalition enables them to stand together, to speak with one voice on the issue and to exert greater influence than possible through individual efforts alone. The International Campaign to Ban Landmines, for example, served as an umbrella organization representing over a thousand NGOs at the Ottawa Conference. Similarly, a coalition of NGOs has been formed concerning the establishment of an International Criminal Court. In order to preserve its neutrality, the ICRC does not formally align itself with coalitions, although it may exchange ideas with the NGOs involved or add its voice to their position. In the context of anti-personal landmines, for example, a group of six NGOs started a campaign calling for their total ban. One year after this inception, the ICRC lent its support to the campaign, thereby bringing to it a credibility that encouraged other, more conservative entities, to come on board, such as religious organizations and the Secretariat of the United Nations.

Finally, if individual efforts or co-operation between NGOs proves unsuccessful, recourse to public opinion may be warranted. Consider again the movement against anti-personal landmines, where collaboration among non-governmental entities alone proved insufficient. States had been using these weapons for decades and therefore had a strong interest in keeping them. It was believed that public opinion would have to be mobilized for the campaign to gain the momentum necessary to succeed. In addition to contacting the press on the issue, therefore, the ICRC, for the first time in its history, considered launching an advertising campaign. This proposed media campaign raised a controversy of opinion within the organization: on the one hand, those opposed to the idea of an ICRC engaged in advertisement, and on the other, those who considered such recourse inevitable, and indeed, highly beneficial, in the light of the global influence the media would yield. In the end, the campaign did take place and, in retrospect, this public approach made the difference.

Non-governmental entities select from these various activities during the pre-diplomatic conference stage; yet specific strategies vary. NGOs tend to raise the stakes by moving straight away from fact-finding to public denunciation. In contrast, because the ICRC deals with governments in the first instance, it always begins with fact-finding and normal bilateral contact with States. Only if these traditional methods prove futile will the ICRC proceed to approach the press, and only then if it believes that this will be beneficial to the victims of the problem. Finally, only exceptional circumstances will result in recourse to public advertisement.

During the Diplomatic Conference

At the diplomatic conference stage, the ICRC has traditionally enjoyed a privileged position compared with NGOs. Not only has the ICRC been granted official access to plenary sessions and working groups, but it has also been given the right to speak directly to delegations, to issue official statements at meetings and, particularly in the context of the 1980 CCW Convention, to submit proposals. On a number of occasions, the organization was asked, in effect, to act as expert rapporteur. Take for instance the negotiations on conventional weapons, where the ICRC was requested to prepare documents discussing possible alternate courses of action on landmines. As a result, the Committee was so heavily solicited by States on technical issues, it organized an informational meeting for interested delegations.

During the diplomatic conference, the ICRC also distributes other material it considers useful, such as a brochure summarizing a more substantial piece of work. NGOs do the same, although they are usually unable to do so formally. Though not frequently allowed into the conference room, the NGOs seek to influence the meetings and communicate their positions by leaving their own material outside to be picked up by State delegations. Past experience shows that such distribution of material is more effective than one may think, for diplomats tend to avail themselves of these leaflets if aware of them.

In addition to providing written material, non-governmental entities, the ICRC and NGOs alike, directly contact State representatives in between sessions and also arrange their own meetings, often by way of press briefings or conferences. These meetings are well attended by States, a further indication that the States indeed take the activities of non-governmental entities very seriously.

Press coverage of the diplomatic conference is also of certain significance. In many conferences, the press is allowed at plenary meetings only and not elsewhere – as in the 1980 CCW Convention negotiations in which, at the request of one State, non-plenary sessions were officially closed. Such exclusions create multiple layers of statements issued by governments. At those meetings that are "open" to the press, for instance, State representatives all express their support for humanitarian goals. Once behind the door, however, where the actual persuasion and debate begin, real and difficult differences of opinion are voiced.

The extent to which NGOs, despite their exclusion from closed meetings, manage to find out details of the discussion is astonishing. However, NGO findings tend to be based, as does the press coverage, on rumours that are sometimes quite incorrect. This is one major disadvantage of closed meetings. Within the context of the conventional weapons debate, for example, several States in favour of restriction on anti-personal landmines were quoted by the press as opponents, a false reportage that drew strong reactions from States. By comparison, meetings at the Ottawa conference were open to the press as well as NGOs, and therefore did not suffer the adverse consequences of rumour-making. Other arrangements similarly protected against erroneous reporting, such as the press row permitted throughout the proceedings. Further, the International Campaign to Ban Landmines, an umbrella organization representing over a thousand NGOs, was given the right to be present in meetings and, like the ICRC, the privilege to speak and make informal proposals.

Concluding Remarks on the Future of NGOs: The Prospect at Rome

The upcoming UN Conference on the Establishment of an International Criminal Court at Rome may illustrate the ambiguity surrounding the future role of non-governmental entities in multilateral treaty-making. A series of meetings of expert governmental representatives has been held, in which the role of non-governmental entities at the Rome conference was debated. As has been the case at the previous diplomatic conferences held in Geneva, the ICRC will assume the official role of Observer in Rome, with the requisite right to be present and speak at all stages of the negotiations. An initial move to exclude NGOs specifically from the formal proceedings was later dropped, due to numerous protests by NGOs and governments. According to the current arrangement of the conference – which may change subsequently and is therefore not final – NGOs will be permitted to be present and participate in meetings informally, but will not be allowed to take the floor or speak in any formal capacity.

In conclusion, there is no doubt that non-governmental entities have a major effect on encouraging a treaty process and on the outcome of the treaty itself. As such, they ensure that the negotiations are not based purely on political pragmatic interests, but also reflect the desire of civil society to achieve as concrete and progressive a result as possible. It is encouraging that State representatives do take the views of civil society seriously, even if the result is not always that which the non-governmental entities would have liked. However, there can be no doubt that their influence has been mostly beneficial and actually appreciated by the majority of States.

PETER MALANCZUK

Multinational Enterprises and Treaty-Making – A Contribution to the Discussion on Non-State Actors and the "Subjects" of International Law

INTRODUCTION

At the outset I would like to record that I was very pleased to be invited to speak on a topic relating to multinational companies.[1] This is so because one of the major research projects of the new Institute of Globalization, International Economic Law and Dispute Settlement (*GLODIS*) at the Erasmus University Rotterdam concerns the status of multinational companies under international law.[2] A closer look,

[1] Generally on the international legal aspects of multinational companies see, for example, D. Kokkini-Iatridou and P.J.I.M. de Waart, "Foreign Investments in Developing Countries – Legal Personality of Multinationals in International Law" (1983) 14 *Netherlands Yearbook of International Law,* pp. 87-131; P. Fisher, "Transnational Enterprises", in R. Bernhardt (ed.), Vol. 8 (1985), *Encyclopedia of Public International Law,* pp. 515-19; A.A. Fatouros, "National Legal Persons in International Law", *ibid.*, Vol. 10 (1987), pp. 299-306; I. Seidl-Hohenveldern, *Corporations in and under International Law*, 1987; *United Nations Centre on Transnational Corporations, Transnational Corporations in World Development: Trends and Prospects*, 1988; P. Mercial, *Les Entreprises multinationales en droit international*, 1993; R. Higgins, "International Law and Foreign Corporations", in *New Diplomacy in the Post Cold War World: Essays for Susan Strange*, 1993; A.A. Fatouros (ed.), *Transnational Corporations: The International Legal Framework*, 1994; D.W. Bachmann, "Transnational Corporations", in R. Wolfrum (ed.), *United Nations: Law, Policies and Practice*, Vol. 2, 1995, pp. 1239-47; P.T. Muchlinski, *Multinational Enterprises and the Law*, 1995; Surya P. Subedi, "Foreign Investment and Sustainable Development", in Weiss, Denters and Waart (eds.), *International Economic Law with a Human Face*, 1998, pp. 413-428; Thomas L. Brewer and Stephen Young, *The Multilateral Investment System and Multinational Enterprises*, 1998, with further references.

[2] The Institute was established in September 1998. For information see the *GLODIS Constitutive Document*, which may be obtained from the Secretariat, GLODIS, Erasmus University Rotterdam, Faculty of Law, Burg. Oudlaan 50, NL-3062 PA Rotterdam, The Netherlands, fax: +31-10-212 5441, e-mail: Glodis@law.eur.nl., website: www.eur.nl/glodis. The Project Manager of the multinationals project is Dr. Menno Kamminga. For the results of a GLODIS conference see M. Kamminga and S. Zia-Zarifi (eds.), *Corporate Liability under International Law* (Kluwer Law International, Dordrecht, 2000).

V. Gowlland-Debbas (ed.), Multilateral Treaty-making, 45–72.

however, revealed that the particular theme "multinational enterprises and treaty-making" appears to be almost a non-topic. It seems that multinational enterprises, at least *de lege lata,* hardly have a formal role to play in international law, apart from the largely unsuccessful attempts of States to treat them as objects of international regulation. They are actors that barely exist on the formal level of international law. Nevertheless, recently a vivid discussion has emerged on the decline of the State in international relations and international law and on the emergence (or enhanced role) of so-called non-State actors, including such diverse entities as international organizations, non-governmental organizations (NGOs), minorities, indigenous peoples, and last not least, multinational enterprises. The discussion often centres on the issue of whether and to what extent they may be regarded as "subjects" of international law.[3]

The following analysis is focusing upon the role of multinational companies in international treaty-making in the sense of public international law. It excludes the discussion of approaches arguing that multinational companies may be seen as genuine law-makers on the global level in another sense, namely in the form of creating a "proto-law" emerging from intrafirm contracts, voluntary codes of conduct and business law practices leading to a global *lex mercatoria.*[4] The paper first outlines the role of multinational enterprises in the international legal system, their position in the global economy, the attempts at international regulation of their activities and the conceptual issues relating to the discussion of whether they are "subjects" of international law. The role of multinational companies in treaty-making will then be discussed under three main aspects. The first aspect to be taken into consideration concerns their role in the conclusion of treaties. This includes the controversial issue of whether certain types of investment agreements concluded between a host State and a foreign company, so-called "internationalized contracts" (or State contracts), constitute a treaty under international law and

---

3 See P. Malanczuk, "Minorities and Self-Determination: Reflections on International Law in General, Including Some Recent Developments in Ethiopia", in Neri Sybesma-Knol/Jef Van Bellingen (eds.), *Naar een nieuwe interpretatie van het Recht op Zelfbeschikking*, 1995, pp. 169-193; Malanczuk, *Akehurst's Modern Introduction to International Law*, 7th rev. ed., 1997, pp. 71-90, 91-108; Malanczuk, "Actors: States, International Organizations, Private Entities", in G. Lafferanderie/Daphné Crowther (eds.), *Outlook on Outer Space Law over the Next 30 Years. Essays published for the 30th Anniversary of the Outer Space Treaty*, 1997, pp. 23-36; Malanczuk, "From the Traditional Interstate Order Towards the Law of the Global Community" [Conference Note: Walther-Schücking-Institute of International Law, University of Kiel, Germany, *International Conference on New Non-State Actors as Subjects of International Law*, 25 –28 March 1998] (Zero Issue) (1998) *ILA International Law Forum*, pp. 23-24; Andrea Bianchi, "Globalization of Human Rights: The Role of Non-State Actors", in Gunther Teubner (ed.), *Global Law Without a State*, 1997, pp. 179-212; Lisa Wilder, "Local Futures? From Denunciation to Revalorization of the Indigenous Other", in Teubner (ed.), *ibid.*, pp. 215-256.

4 See the contributions in Gunther Teubner (ed.), *Global Law Without a State*, 1997, by Jean Philippe Robe, "Multinational Enterprises: The Constitution of a Pluralistic Legal Order", pp. 45-77; Peter T. Muchlinski, "'Global Bukowina' Examined: Viewing the Multinational Enterprise as a Transnational Law-making Community", pp. 79-108.

elevate the foreign private investor to a "partial subject" of international law. The second aspect that will be dealt with is the role of multinational companies in the negotiation of treaties, both with regard to their formal consultative status as well as with respect to informal lobbying for their interests. The third aspect addresses the role of multinational companies in the implementation of treaties in the form of making direct use of dispute settlement mechanisms provided for by treaties, followed by some conclusions.

THE ROLE OF MULTINATIONAL ENTERPRISES IN THE INTERNATIONAL LEGAL SYSTEM

Definition of Multinational Enterprises and Role in the Global Economy

There are the numerous and controversial definitions of multinational enterprises or so-called transnational corporations (TNCs).[5] For the purposes of this paper it suffices to use the broad definition employed by the OECD Guidelines on Multinational Enterprises that in essence was subsequently also adopted by the UN Draft Code of Conduct on Transnational Enterprises. According to this definition, multinational enterprises

> "usually comprise companies or other entities whose ownership is private, State or mixed, established in different countries and so linked that one or more of them may be able to exercise a significant influence over the activities of others, and, in particular, to share knowledge and resources with the others."[6]

The emergence of modern transnational companies reflects the globalization of economic activities and new forms of specialization and the international division of labour requiring direct investment in foreign markets. It is well known that multinational enterprises play an important role in the world economy and are the driving forces of the process of economic globalization.[7] The global network of production is primarily based upon the transnational activities of such companies. The turnover and wealth of these multinationals are growing faster than the world social product. In the richest 14 industrial countries the number of transnational companies has risen from 7000 in 1969 to about 24,000 in 1994. Globally, there

---

[5] See Muchlinski, *Multinational Enterprises, op. cit.*, pp. 12-15; Brewer and Young, *The Multilateral Investment System, op. cit.*, p. 11 *et seq.*

[6] OECD Guidelines for Multinational Enterprises, 21 June 1976, introduction, para. 8; Draft UN Code of Conduct for TNCs, UN Doc. E/1990/94, 12 June 1990, para. 1, at 5.

[7] See P. Malanczuk, "Globalization and the Future Role of Sovereign States", in Friedl Weiss, Eric Denters and Paul de Waart (eds.), *International Economic Law with a Human Face*, 1998, pp. 45-65. The following section is based on a revised part of this article.

are currently between 37,000[8] and 44,000[9] multinational companies (depending on definitions and sources) with about 280,000 subsidiaries. Meanwhile, the 100 largest companies (measured by the amount of foreign property) control one-fifth of the participation capital globally invested. Among the top twelve companies, led by Shell/Royal Dutch based in the United Kingdom and the Netherlands, there are five based in the United States (Ford, General Electric, Exxon, General Motors and IBM), two in Germany (Volkswagen and Bayer), two in Japan (Toyota and Mitsubishi) and two in Switzerland (Nestlé and ABB). There are only two companies (listed for the first time) among the top 100 that are based in emerging economies: Daewoo (Korea) and Petroleos de Venezuela, ranked as numbers 52 and 88 respectively. However, there are some new developments indicating that multinational enterprises from Third World countries are increasing their foreign investment in other developing countries by locating their technology and know-how in industrialized countries.[10]

It is also interesting to note that the companies with the strongest international orientation are not based in the great trading nations of the United States, Japan or Germany, but rather in States with small domestic markets. If one follows the globalization index of UNCTAD, which does not rely upon absolute figures, but on foreign shares with regard to property, turnover and employment,[11] then the Swiss food company Nestlé is on the top of the list, although its foreign investment is smaller than that of Shell. Under this index, Nestlé is followed by the Canadian publishing company Thomson and the Swiss Holderbank group, the world's largest cement producer.

About one third of world trade takes place within groups of such companies which are increasingly organizing themselves in the form of global networks and "strategic alliances". This implies that rather diverse local sites may be advantageous for different stages of the production process and the various phases of the production cycle. Catchwords such as "outsourcing" and "global sourcing" are labels to describe the method of companies to transfer parts of their production to other countries and regions of the world to take advantage of lower wages and lower costs of real estate.[12] The production process thus becomes internationalized and optimized.

---

8 T. Bernauer, "Weltpolitik im 21. Jahrhundert: kein 'Vorwärts' in die Vergangenheit – Von den Grenzen der Globalisierung" (1997) 45 *Vereinte Nationen*, p. 50.

9 UNCTAD, *World Investment Report,* 1997.

10 See John H. Dunning, Roger van Hoesel and Rajneesh Narula, "Third World Multinationals Revisited: New Developments and Theoretical Implications", in John H. Dunning (ed.), *Globalization, Trade and Foreign Direct Investment*, 1998, pp. 255-286. See also C. Souza, "Latin America's Emerging Multinationals", *Financial Times*, Part 10 of "Mastering Global Business", 3 April 1998, p. 8.

11 See *Frankfurter Allgemeine Zeitung* of 22 September 1997, p. 15.

12 H.-O. Henkel, "Globalisierung der Wirtschaft: eine Herausforderung für die internationale Gemeinschaft" (1995) 43 *Vereinte Nationen*, p. 194.

The most important factor of the globalization of the economy is foreign direct investment by companies in foreign markets. The dramatic increase in such capital movements since the mid 1980s, with a brief interruption in 1992-93, indicates that transnational enterprises are becoming more and more important. It is expected that foreign direct investment will continue to grow significantly over the next five years, leading to stronger integration of the world economy.[13] Foreign investment is primarily driven by the motive to obtain market access and only secondarily by the interest in benefiting from lower wage costs abroad. In 1996 total foreign direct investment reached the record figure of $ 349 billion. Capital imports by which foreign companies made acquisitions were 10% higher than in 1995. This growth rate exceeded the growth rates of world production and international trade. Company take-overs and mergers, mainly in the United States and Europe, accounted for almost half of foreign direct investment.

It is important to note that industrialized countries still take the lion's share of this transfer of capital; however, the distance to developing countries is shrinking. In 1996, developing countries registered a record inflow of $ 129 billion, a share of 34%. Most foreign direct investment again went to China and, significantly less, to Brazil, Singapore and Indonesia. There was less foreign direct investment in Eastern Europe (about $ 12 billion) because of the reduced process of privatization.

It is often argued that these huge multinational companies have largely escaped regulatory control by States because they are able to select countries offering them the most favorable terms as regards, for example, taxes, environmental standards and social legislation.[14] For example, Paul Kennedy notes that the multinational corporations have "more global reach than global responsibility". He states that "'the real logic' of the borderless world is that nobody is in control – except, perhaps, the managers of multinational corporations, whose responsibility is to their shareholders, who, one might argue, have become the new sovereigns, investing in whatever company gives the highest returns.[15] Indeed, in recent years, the gospel of "shareholder value" has become a major point of orientation in business operations and management, although the principle may be more attractive than its actual practice.[16] Apart from perceived challenges to State sovereignty emanating from functions taken over by the United Nations and other international organizations and from a proliferation of supranational regional organizations, some authors mention the unprecedented privatization of State functions in industrialized States, former socialist States and developing countries as a third possible challenge.[17]

---

[13] UNCTAD, *World Investment Report*, 1997.

[14] See, for example, Vivien A. Schmidt, "The New World Order, Incorporated: The Rise of Business and the Decline of the Nation-State" (1995) 124 *Daedalus (Journal of the American Academy of Arts and Sciences)*, pp. 75-106.

[15] Paul Kennedy, *Preparing for the Twenty-First Century*, 1993, p. 55.

[16] See *Financial Times* of 27 October 1997, p. 12.

[17] Karl M. Meessen, "Sovereignty", in R. Wolfrum (ed.), *United Nations: Law, Policies and Practice*, Vol. 2, 1995, p. 1199.

Referring to the theoretical concept of the "minimal State"(Robert Nozick), Karl M. Meessen takes the following view:

> "Once the means of production are privatized world-wide, once trade in goods and services is liberalized, once all State owned and State licensed monopolies are dismantled, and once macroeconomic decision-making is entrusted to market forces alone, the question arises whether the State deprived of all those functions will continue 'to be above' all private forces that might emerge by then. For example, multinational enterprises, whose earlier challenge to State sovereignty had been overcome in the 1970s, might then escape another reinforcement of State control."[18]

Such views seem to be reinforced by the wave of mergers between big companies that hit a record level in 1998. There were mergers valuing $2.4 trillion world-wide, a 50% increase on 1997, itself a record year. The merger wave included the $80 billion merger announced between the oil giants Exxon and Mobil. Cross-border deals accounted for a quarter of the world-wide company mergers in 1998, including Daimler-Benz's take-over of Chrysler and the take-over of Bankers Trust by Deutsche Bank.[19] When the world's largest financial services group was formed in 1998 between Travellers and Citicorp, it is reported that at one point in the merger discussions a director asked the question: "Can anybody stop us?". After a short silence, someone suggested "NATO".[20] However, one needs to bear in mind that for a number of reasons, including differences in corporate culture, such mergers of large companies have often failed in the past.

It is true that States find it difficult to regulate effectively on the national level the activities of global companies. This is due to the corporations' extensive network of decision-making and operational structures formed by their headquarters, branches, subsidiaries and other forms of investment in independent company units throughout the world. It is also due to their flexibility in moving seats of production as well as moving profits within the framework of the organization as a whole.

Nevertheless, the general power relationship between States and multinational companies is more complicated than it may appear at first sight. For example, one would need to distinguish between the interests of the host States and the interests of the home States of such companies. Moreover, the following arguments need to be taken into account. First, although there is a trend towards globalization, global companies are in fact operating in a world economy that is not fully integrated and in an global political system in which States adopt national regulatory and other policies according to their own interests which often have international or extraterritorial consequences.[21] Second, only few transnational companies produce more than one-fifth of their products in foreign countries. Multinational companies depend on the availability of a reliable public infrastructure. As such infrastructure is

---

18 *Ibid.*, p. 1200.

19 See *The Economist* of 9 January 1999, pp. 19-21.

20 *Ibid.*, at 19.

21 See Edward M. Graham, *Global Corporations and National Governments*, 1996.

to a large extent provided by the State, this also makes them subject to State regulation.[22] Third, multinational companies not only require diplomatic protection in many instances, but also need States to conclude international agreements with rules in many different areas of international economic law to achieve legal certainty and predictability for international business transactions. This includes the important international financial framework and monetary system underling international trade and investment.[23] It further includes the multilateral framework for international trade and investment provided under the umbrellas of GATT/WTO and regional economic arrangements. And it finally includes the network of some 1300 bilateral investment treaties that have been concluded between capital-exporting States and capital-importing States to protect the private foreign investor with the establishment of adequate international dispute settlement mechanisms and clear rules on expropriation and standard of compensation.[24] It is therefore unlikely that States will lose regulatory control over large areas of the global economy.

The problems arising from the sheer volume, speed and effects of trading on the international financial markets are far more serious. In this respect, it can be reasonably stated that the development of "virtual money" (not backed by real economic activity, but arising from speculation on profits from currency exchange differences) has moved beyond the current control of States and the capacity of their central banks to intervene. The enormous funds moving around the globe daily, instantaneously and without regulation can cause a serious dislocation within financial markets with detrimental consequences for the world economy as a whole. The currency problems in Europe in 1992 and 1993, in Mexico in 1994-1995, most recently in East Asia in 1997 (Thailand and Indonesia) and 1998 in Russia and Brazil have given rise to substantial concern.[25]

Again, all of this does not inevitably lead to the conclusion that the State has become powerless even in this complicated area. First, rescue operations in cases of a national currency crisis are undertaken by international State-controlled institutions, such as the IMF, the World Bank and regional development banks, backed up by individual States.[26] Second, States have not lost the power to co-operate and

---

22 See Bernauer, *op. cit.*, pp. 50-51 with further considerations.

23 For details see Malanczuk, *Akehurst's, op. cit.*, ch. 15: (Economy), pp. 222-240 with references to the literature.

24 See Muchlinski, *Multinational Enterprises*, *op. cit.*, p. 617 *et seq.*; R. Dolzer and M. Stevens, *Bilateral Investment Treaties*, 1995; Paul Peters, "Some Serendipitous Findings in BITs: the Barcelona Traction Case and the Reach of Bilateral Investment Treaties", in Erik Denters and Nico Schrijver (eds.), *Reflections on International Law from the Low Countries in Honour of Paul de Waart*, 1998, pp. 27-47.

25 See Philip G. Cerny, "International Finance and the Erosion of State Policy Capacity", in Philip Gummett (ed.), *Globalization and Public Policy*, 1996, pp. 83-104.

26 In the recent case of Indonesia, the loans granted by the IMF, World Bank and the Asian Development Bank in the amount of $23 billion were supported by additional offers from the United States, Japan, Singapore, Malaysia with more expected from Australia, Hong Kong and perhaps China, see *Financial Times* of 3 November 1997, p. 18. It is inter-

agree on more efficient international institutions and instruments to stabilize the international financial system.

There is some evidence that the regulatory and economic policy-making capacity of States (i.e. by changing taxation, interest rates, currency exchange rates or introducing exchange controls) to act autonomously has diminished in certain areas since the 1980s.[27] But States still have considerable scope of action within their own territory and the ability to recover by multilateral co-operation many of the powers they may have lost.[28] The proposition that the global economy will be dominated by only two forces, that of the market and that of multinational enterprises,[29] appears as highly exaggerated. In sum, an empirical investigation into the discernible effects of globalization shows that the alleged decline and retreat of the State facing world market forces is rather overrated and this is so mainly for political and ideological reasons.[30]

Moreover, another circumstance needs to be taken into account when assessing the relative power of multinational companies. This is the role of "civil society" and the influence of pressure groups that hold global companies responsible for the world's evils: for environmental destruction and pollution, for the exploitation of children and the violation of democratic and human rights.[31] Sections of public opinion throughout the world are fearful of the process of globalization and suspicious of giant companies, which appear to be beyond the control of States.[32] Often pressure groups choose multinational companies concerned about their public relations as a target to remedy grievances where pressure on governments leads to no immediate result.

Attempts at International Regulation of the Activities of Multinational Enterprises

Some States, for obvious economic reasons, are more favorable to the operations of multinational companies based in their own territory than other States where these companies are operating. In the past especially developing countries have ex-

---

esting to note in this connection that Mr. Robert Rubin, US Treasury secretary, stated the following: "Financial stability around the world is critical to the national security and economic interests of the United States", *ibid.*, p. 16.

27 See Bernauer, *op. cit.*, p. 50.

28 *Report of a High-level Expert Group on Opportunities and Risks of Globalization, chaired by Lord Callaghan of Cardiff, 18th-20th March 1997, Washington, D.C.*, Communiqué of the InterAction Council, 15th Session, 1-4 June 1997, Noordwijk, Netherlands, 2.

29 David C. Korten, *When Corporations Rule the World*, 1995.

30 See the illuminating analysis in the special supplement: The future of the State. A survey of the world economy, *The Economist* of 20 September 1997.

31 See *Financial Times* of 31 October 1997, 15. On the historical background see the summary given by Menno Kamminga, "Aansprakelijkheid van (multinationale) ondernemingen voor schendingen van internationaal recht" (1997) 22 NJCM-Bulletin, p. 785.

32 See, for example, from a trade union point of view, Detlef Hensche, "Armut, Vertreibung, Umweltzerstörung anderswo – was geht uns das an? – Von der Notwendigkeit solidarischen Ausgleichs in einer kleiner werdenden Welt" (1995) 43 *Vereinte Nationen*, pp. 196-200.

pressed concern about the dominance of TNCs in national economies, in contract negotiations and in other respects concerning company interests, including interference in the domestic politics of the host State. Industrialized countries, on the other hand, tend to be more worried about the protection of the investments of their multinationals in foreign countries and about legal certainty for their transactions. This discussion on the international level has been closely related to the dispute in the 1960s and 1970s on the programme, advanced by developing countries, for a New International Economic Order (NIEO), and on the expropriation of foreign property and the required standard of compensation.[33]

With regard to the activities of multinational enterprises, various international bodies have been engaged in finding a compromise by formulating so-called codes of conduct of a recommendatory nature, for example the International Chamber of Commerce, the International Labour Organization and the OECD.[34] Of particular importance have been the protracted negotiations in the United Nations since 1977 on a UN Draft Code of Conduct on Transnational Corporations and the work of the UN Centre on TNCs.[35] The issue has meanwhile lost much of its former political significance, since a number of developing countries now have transnational companies of their own and almost all of them have become more interested in the flow of private foreign investment into their economies, and because of the changes in the former socialist countries after the end of the Cold War. Significantly, following the shift in 1993 of the UN programme on TNCs from New York to UNCTAD in Geneva,[36] in 1994 ECOSOC installed the renamed Commission on International Investment and TNCs as an advisory body to the Trade and Development Board.[37] Attempts, promoted especially by developing countries, to regulate the activities of multinational companies on the international level by non-binding "codes of conduct" have thus produced little result and, due to changed economic and political circumstances, are no longer a matter of political relevance.

---

33 See Malanczuk, *Akehurst's*, *op. cit.*, p. 233 *et seq.* with references; Thomas W. Waelde, "A Requiem for the 'New International Economic Order' – The Rise and Fall of Paradigms in International Economic Law and a Post-Mortem with Timeless Significance", in G. Hafner, G. Loibl, A. Rest, L. Sucharipa-Behrmann and K. Zemanek (eds.), *Liber Amicorum Professor Ignaz Seidl-Hohenveldern – in Honour of his 80th birthday*, 1998, pp. 771-804.

34 See, for example, the 1976 OECD Declaration on International Investment and Multinational Enterprises, Guidelines for Multinational Enterprises (1976) 15 *International Legal Materials*, p. 15 *et seq.*, and the 1977 ILO Tripartite Declaration of Principles concerning Multilateral Enterprises and Social Policy (1978) 17 *International Legal Materials*, p. 422 *et seq.* See further E.-U. Petersmann, "Codes of Conduct", in R. Bernhardt (ed.), *Encyclopedia of Public International Law*, Vol. I (1992), pp. 627-32. Seymour J. Rubin, "Transnational Corporations and International Codes of Conduct: A Study of the Relationship between International Legal Cooperation and Economic Development" (1995) 10 *American University Journal of International Law and Policy*, pp. 1275-1289.

35 On the drafts see (1984) 23 *International Legal Materials*, p. 626; (1989) 4 ICSID Review, p. 135. See W. Spröte, "Negotiations on a United Nations Code of Conduct on Transnational Corporations" (1990) 33 *German Yearbook of International Law*, p. 331.

36 (1993) 4 *Yearbook of International Environmental Law*, p. 103.

37 (1994) 5 *Yearbook of International Environmental Law*, p. 136.

In sum, it appears that multinational enterprises hardly have a role to play in international law, apart from the largely unsuccessful attempts of States to treat them as objects of international regulation, at least *de lege lata*. The question therefore is to which extent multinational companies can be considered to be "subjects of international law".

Multinational Enterprises as "Subjects" of International Law

Conceptual Issues

First, it is appropriate to clarify some conceptual issues.[38] The statement that an entity is a "subject" of international law is mostly used interchangeably with the determination that it is a "legal person" under international law.[39] It means that it has a capacity to enter into legal relations and to have legal rights and duties. In the nineteenth century, under the influence of the then prevailing positivist doctrine, States had become the only legal persons in international law. Writing in 1912, in his famous treatise on international law, L. Oppenheim still found: "Since the law of nations is based on the common consent of individual States, and not of individual human beings, States solely and exclusively are subjects of international law."[40] While States have remained the predominant actors in international law, the position has changed in the last century. Other actors, such as international organizations and individuals are considered to have also acquired some degree of international legal personality; however, the precise extent of the legal personality they have acquired has remained rather controversial.

From a conceptual point of view, it is important to note that legal personality is primarily related to the capacity to bring claims arising from the violation of international law, to conclude valid international agreements, and to enjoy privileges and immunities from national jurisdictions.[41] The International Court of Justice has observed that "[t]he subjects of law in any legal system are not necessarily identical in their nature or in the extent of their rights, and their nature depends upon the needs of the community".[42] It is the international legal system that determines

---

38 This section is based on a revised version of the relevant text in Malanczuk, *Akehurst's*, *op. cit.*, pp. 92-93.

39 The *Restatement (Third) of the Foreign Relations Law of the United States*, Vol. 1, part II, 1987, p. 70, dealing with "persons in international law", however, rejects the term "subjects" because it may have more limited implications meaning that such entities have only rights and duties, and not also, to varying extents, legal status and personality under international law. See further H. Mosler, "Subjects of International Law", in R. Bernhardt (ed.), *Encyclopedia of Public International Law,* Vol. 7 (1984), pp. 442-59; J.A. Barberis, *Los sujetos del derecho internacional actual*, 1984; P.K. Menon, "The Subjects of Modern International Law" (1990) 3 *Hague Yearbook of International Law*, pp. 30-86; I. Brownlie, *Principles of Public International Law*, 4th edn 1990, p. 58 *et seq.*; Conference on Changing Notions of Sovereignty and the Role of Private Actors in International Law, (1993-4) 9 *American University Journal of International Politics and Law,* pp. 1-213.

40 L. Oppenheim, *International Law. A Treatise*, 2nd ed. 1912, Vol. I (Peace), p. 19.

41 Ian Brownlie, *Principles of Public International Law*, *op. cit.*, p. 58.

42 *Reparations for Injuries Case,* (1949) ICJ Rep., p. 178.

which are the subjects of international law and which kind of legal personality they enjoy on the international level.

Legal personality can be unlimited, in the sense that, in principle, *all* international rights and obligations can be accorded to a subject. This is so only in the case of States, the original, primary and universal subjects of international law. States have exclusive jurisdiction with respect to their territory and personal jurisdiction over their nationals. Other subjects of international law, such as international organizations created by States, have legal personality only with respect to *certain* international rights and obligations. The legal personality of international organizations is limited as to substance by the treaty which States have concluded to constitute them and to accord them rights and duties to achieve their specific tasks. It is also relative in the sense that it exists only with regard to the member States of the organization and with respect to non-member States acknowledging the organization. Such secondary subjects act *ultra vires*, meaning that their acts are legally void, if they operate beyond the authority given to them by the constitutive treaty.[43]

Individuals, on the other hand, have acquired a certain status under international law with the development of human rights[44] and with regard to their criminal liability under international law,[45] but they cannot make treaties or create rules of customary international law. Thus, one can say that individuals have some degree of international legal personality; but the personality is much more limited than the legal personality of international organizations. Individuals may have various rights under special treaties, for instance, but it has never been suggested that they can imitate States by acquiring territory, appointing ambassadors, or declaring war. As in the case of international organizations, it is therefore useless to treat legal personality as an absolute concept; one must break it down into specific rights and duties. The same applies to the case of multinational enterprises.

The international legal personality of individuals and companies (and, indeed, of international organizations) is still comparatively rare and limited. Moreover, it is derivative, in the sense that it can be conferred only by States. It is States which set up international organizations; it is States which make treaties or adopt customary rules giving international rights to individuals and companies; it is only States (or international organizations, created by States) which can make contracts with

---

43 See F. Morgenstern, "Legality in International Organizations" (1976-7) 48 *British Yearbook of International Law*, pp. 241-258; E. Osieke, "Ultra Vires Acts in International Organizations – The Experience of the International Labour Organization", *ibid.*, pp. 259-280.

44 C.A. Norgaard, *The Position of the Individual in International Law*, 1962; R.A. Mullerson, "Human Rights and the Individual as a Subject of International Law" (1990) I *European Journal of International Law*, pp. 33-43; K.J. Partsch, "Individuals in International Law", in R. Bernhardt (ed.), *Encyclopedia of Public International Law*, Vol. II (1995), pp. 957-962; P.K. Menon, "The Legal Personality of Individuals" (1994) 6 *Sri Lanka Journal of International Law*, pp. 127-156;.

45 See Malanczuk, *Akehurst's*, p. 353 *et seq.* with references.

individuals or companies governed by international law. Consequently, when some States say that individuals are subjects of international law, and when other States disagree, both sides may be right. If States in the first group confer international rights on individuals, then individuals are subjects of international law as far as those States are concerned. States in the second group can, for practical purposes, prevent individuals from acquiring international personality, by refraining from giving them any rights that are valid under international law. The same is true for multinational enterprises.

The Position of Multinational Enterprises

The general status of multinational enterprises under current international law may be described as follows. In spite of an increasing recognition of a certain international subjectivity for private natural and legal persons, multinational enterprises are still denied "full international personality". This is so because they lack the power to directly participate in the international law-making process, which is seen as one of the main attributes attached to that status.[46] In discussing non-State actors as " subjects" of international law and objects of regulation and the relevant codes of conduct, Baade, for example, notes that multinational enterprises are

> "neither States nor public international organizations, and thus neither 'natural' nor 'artificial' subjects of international law as presently defined. Even if their procedural role in follow-up proceedings should, in analogy to human-rights complaint mechanisms suffice to confer upon them 'partial' or *ad hoc* international subjectivity, they would still lack at least one of the essential attributes of full international personality. This is the power to participate directly in the international norm-creating process. It follows that the practice of MNEs in response to codes of conduct or guidelines, quite irrespective of its motivations, cannot supply the element of *opinio necessitatis iuris* that remains an indispensable prerequisite for the development of customary international law."[47]

In this sense, the Third Restatement of US Foreign Relations Law also notes:

> "The multinational enterprise or corporation (sometimes referred to as a transnational or global corporation) is an established feature of international economic life, but it has not yet achieved special status in international law or in domestic legal systems."[48]

---

[46] Hans W. Baade, "The Legal Effects of Codes of Conduct", in Norbert Horn (ed.), *Legal Problems of Codes of Conduct for Multinational Enterprises*, 1980, p. 8.

[47] Baade, *ibid.*, reprinted in Fatouros (ed.), *Transnational Corporations*, *op. cit.*, pp. 212-250, at 215.

[48] Vol. 1, 1987, p. 126, see also 130 (Reporter's Notes). Malcom N. Shaw, *International Law*, 4th ed., 1997, pp. 176-177, notes that if an international code of conduct for multinational corporations would come into effect, imposing direct duties on companies as well as ascribing rights to them against the host State, "it would be possible to regard them as international persons". He states that this, however, has not yet happened. A discussion of

Sauvant and Aranda also emphasize that multinational enterprises

> "are not recognized as independent subjects of international law; despite their international economic impact, in legal terms they remain under the sovereignty of the States in which they operate."[49]

Even the influential group of the few outstanding global multinational companies (such as IBM, ITT or Unilever), which already hold more economic and political power than many States and, in connection with the globalization of the economy under the communications and financial revolution, are likely to become stronger still in the next century,[50] have not been upgraded by States to international subjects proper.[51] States prefer to maintain control over these corporations, rather than accepting them on a legally equal footing, although, as noted above, it is often difficult in practice to effectively regulate on the national level the activities of such global companies.

This general lack of formal recognition of the existence of multinational companies as actors on the international plane within the system of international law is reflected in their rather limited role in international treaty-making.

The Role of Multinational Enterprises in the Conclusion of Treaties

The General Position of Multinational Enterprises in the Formal Conclusion of Treaties

In discussing the role of multinational enterprises in the formal conclusion of treaties, certain distinctions need to be made at the outset. On the one hand, it is quite clear that international business contracts entered into between private companies located in different States (disregarding the vexed problem of determining the proper nationality of multinational companies) are not treaties in the sense of public international law. They are private law agreements subject to the rules and principles of one or another national legal system, or what – somewhat misleadingly – is called private international law.

On the other hand, it is also clear that bilateral or multilateral treaties under public international law can only be concluded among the subjects of international law, such as States, international organizations or other recognized subjects of international law. Generally speaking, multinational companies have no formal role to play in this respect. They cannot sign or ratify a multilateral treaty, or later ac-

---

this proposition is not necessary in the present context because the analysis is limited to the role of multinational companies in treaty-making.

49 K.P. Sauvant and V. Aranda, "The International Legal Framework for Transnational Corporations", in Fatouros (ed.), *Transnational Corporations*, *op. cit.*, pp. 83-115, at 84.

50 See Kennedy, *Preparing for the Twenty-First Century*, *op. cit.*, ch. 3.

51 A. Cassese, *International Law in a Divided World*, 1986, p. 103.

cede to it as a party. The same generally applies to bilateral treaties under international law. However, there is a special area where this is disputed relating to the phenomenon of so-called "internationalized contracts".

The Case of "Internationalized Contracts"

The term "internationalized contracts" refers to agreements concluded between States and foreign companies (often also called "State contracts"),[52] particularly in the field of oil concessions or development agreements,[53] allowing a foreign private enterprise to explore and exploit natural resources on the territory of the State. They have given rise to a controversy on whether such agreements may be considered as treaties under international law, with the consequence that multinational corporations, at least to some degree, may acquire the status of subjects of international law.

According to their applicable law clause, such "internationalized contracts" are not governed by a certain national legal system, such as that of the host State, but by international law. The contract is to be governed by general principles of law, general principles of the law of nations, principles of the law of the State party not inconsistent with international law, or only by the provisions of the contract itself. The purpose is to establish a balance between the parties and ensure that the State party cannot evade its obligations under the contract by manipulating its own internal law. Furthermore, other clauses may be included, such as "implementation clauses", declaring that the contract will be implemented in the host State's national legal system, or "stabilization clauses", stipulating that the financial, economic or legal conditions existing at the time of the conclusion of the agreement will not be altered for the period of the contract. In addition, such contracts mostly contain an arbitration clause referring disputes under the agreement to an international body, rather than to the national courts of the host State.[54]

---

[52] R. Jennings, "State Contracts in International Law" (1961) 32 *British Yearbook of International Law,* p. 156 *et seq.*; K.-H. Böckstiegel, *Der Staat als Vertragspartner ausländischer Privatunternehmen*, 1971; D.W. Bowett, "State Contracts with Aliens: Contemporary Developments on Compensation for Termination or Breach" (1988) 59 *British Yearbook of International Law,* p. 49 *et seq.*; E. Paasivirta, "Internationalization and Stabilization of Contracts versus State Sovereignty", *ibid.*, (1989) 60, p. 315 *et seq.*; M. Sornarajah, *International Commercial Arbitration: The Protection of State Contracts*, 1990; G.v. Hecke, "Contracts between States and Foreign Private Law Persons", in R. Bernhardt (ed.), *Encyclopedia of Public International Law*, Vol. I (1992), pp. 814-19; see also v. Hecke, "Contracts between International Organizations and Private Law Persons", *ibid.*, pp. 812-14; A.F.M. Maniruzzaman, "State Contracts with Aliens. The Question of Unilateral Change by the State in Contemporary International Law" (1992) 9 *Journal of International Arbitration,* pp. 141-71; G.R. Delaume, *Transnational Contracts – Applicable Law and Settlement of Disputes*, 1992.

[53] P. Fisher, Concessions, in R. Bernhardt (ed.), *Encyclopedia of Public International Law*, Vol. I (1992), pp. 715-21; A.Z.E. Chiali, "Protection of Investment in the Context of Petroleum Agreements" 204 *Recueil des cours* (1987-IV), pp. 13-169.

[54] The most important arbitration cases since 1929 are listed in v. Hecke, *op. cit.*

Some developing countries have qualified such clauses as without effect because it would be incompatible with State sovereignty, in particular sovereign rights of the host State over its natural resources.[55] In the (mostly Western) literature, on the other hand, there have been various attempts to arrive at a proper classification of these internationalized contracts, without leading to a consensus.

One view is that the foreign company party to such an internationalized contract becomes a subject of international law, which, however, is considered to be functionally limited. It is based upon the argument that such agreements with the host State concern matters of State functions (i.e. transfer to the foreign company of State tasks, exemptions from legislation, the granting of immunities and privileges similar to those enjoyed by diplomats), thereby entrusting the foreign enterprise with certain international rights and duties.[56] Friedmann already argued in the direction of this so-called *international agreement doctrine* in 1964[57] and there are even much earlier views in support of this view based upon a variety of arguments, including the doctrine of acquired rights and the principle of *pacta sunt servanda*, and references to international decisions.[58] The theory that private foreign investors may thus be partial subjects of international law, limited to the cases of such internationalized contracts, has been particularly advanced by Böckstiegel in 1971[59] and by Dupuy in his decision as arbitrator in the Libyan dispute with American oil companies in 1978.[60] Moreover, in the more recent literature one could also refer to Herdegen[61] and Seidl-Hohenveldern.[62]

Other authors are willing to recognize that multinational companies increasingly are acquiring (partial) status in international law and refer to direct contracts between such companies and States which are seen as an essential characteristic of

---

55 See *Restatement (Third) of the Foreign Relations Law of the United States*, Vol. 2, 1987, p. 214

56 See, for example, Waldemar Hummer, "Internationale und transnationale Akteure an oder unter der Schwelle der Völkerrechtssubjektivität", in Hanspeter Neuhold, Waldemar Hummer and Christoph Schreuer (eds.), *Österreichisches Handbuch des Völkerrechts*, Band 1, 3rd ed., 1997, p. 224; Peter Fischer, "Internationales Wirtschaftsrecht und Internationale Wirtschaftsorganisationen", *ibid.*, p. 440. See also Wildhaber, "International-rechtliche Probleme multilateraler Kooperation" (1978) 18 *Berichte der Deutschen Gesellschaft für Völkerrecht*, p. 7 at 300.

57 Friedmann, *The Changing Structure of International Law*, 1964, pp. 221-231.

58 See the extensive references in Brownlie, *Principles*, *op. cit.*, pp. 547-552.

59 Karl-Heinz Böckstiegel, *Der Staat als Vertragspartner ausländischer Privatunternehmen*, 1971.

60 *Texas Overseas Petroleum Co. & California Asiatic Oil Co. v. Libyan Arab Republic* (1978) 17 *International Legal Materials*, p. 1. Prof. Dupuy's approach did not find uniform support in later arbitral awards, see Muchlinksi, *Multinational Enterprises*, *op. cit.*, p. 494 *et seq.*

61 Matthias Herdegen, *Internationales Wirtschaftsrecht*, 2nd ed., 1995, pp. 205-208; at 58 the author describes this view as an advancing one.

62 I. Seidl-Hohenveldern, *International Economic Law*, 2nd ed., 1992, pp. 10-20.

the international economic order.[63] Vitzthum, for example, qualifies such contracts as "quasi international law", at least giving the appearance of international law, without directly giving multinational companies international rights and duties.[64]

One of the main arguments against the *international agreement doctrine* is that the consent of a single State cannot elevate its private contract partner to a subject (even a partial one) of international law.[65] The international agreement doctrine relies on an analogy drawn from the derivative international legal personality of international organizations and contends that this concept can be also applied to multinational corporations. The deficiency of this analogy is that the international legal personality of an international organization is not constituted by its recognition by a non-member State.[66]This international legal personality derives from the constituent instrument establishing the organization, normally a multilateral treaty concluded among the State parties. Recognition of the international organization by a third State only extends the existing international legal relations of the organization by a constitutive act also to that State. Furthermore, the international agreement doctrine implies that if a State may unilaterally transfer international legal personality to an entity, the same State would be in a position to unilaterally withdraw international legal personality, even if international treaties bind it to the respective subject of international law. This is incompatible with the principle of *pacta sunt servanda*. Finally, international practice also fails to significantly support the international agreement doctrine. The objective element of State practice for the formation of a respective customary international law rule is lacking,[67] even more so absent is the subjective element of *opinio juris*.

At most, therefore, one could argue that, while the contract remains subject to the national legal system of the host State, international law may be applied by way of analogy, based upon the will of the parties.[68] It is true that this construction does not solve the underlying problem from the viewpoint of the foreign investor, because the reference to international law in the agreement, as part of the contract, then remains subject to national law, which may be altered unilaterally by the host State.[69] However, this appears to be inevitable for systemic reasons following from the contemporary basic structure of international law.

---

63 Wolfgang Graf Vitzthum, Begriff, "Geschichte und Quellen des Völkerrechts", in Vitzthum (ed.), *Völkerrecht*, 1997, p. 17.

64 Vitzthum, *ibid.*; see also pp. 96-97 for further considerations.

65 Heintschel von Heinegg, in Knut Ipsen (ed.), *Völkerrecht*, 3rd ed. 1990, pp. 102-103.

66 See V. Epping, "Völkerrechtssubjekte", in Knut Ipsen (ed.), *Völkerrecht, op. cit.*, p. 93.

67 Epping, *ibid.*, also with reference to Liemen, *Erdöl-Produktionsverträge des Iran*, 1981, p. 150 *et seq.*

68 Heintschel von Heinegg, *op. cit.*, p. 103.

69 Wolfgang Graf Vitzthum, "Raum Umwelt und Wirtschaft im Völkerrecht", in Vitzthum (ed.), *Völkerrecht*, *op. cit.*, pp. 503-504, arguing that bilateral investment protec-

Therefore, the traditional view denies that transnational enterprises are subjects of international law, even if they are often equal partners to States in concluding investment agreements or in the conduct of arbitral proceedings.[70] Thus, with regard to the issue of State contracts, the Third Restatement of the Foreign Relations Law of the United States takes "an intermediate view". It accepts the validity of internationalization clauses, enabling courts and tribunals to develop rules for the resolution of disputes under such contracts, without, however, conceding that such clauses render the contract an international agreement, subject, for example, to the remedies of international law.[71]

It is also notable that Ian Brownlie, in his revised version of the General Course on Public International Law delivered at the Hague Academy of International Law in 1995, in dealing with the subjects of international law, does not even mention multinational companies, although he addresses, for example, minorities, indigenous peoples, individuals and international organizations, in addition to States.[72] There is, however, an extensive discussion, with detailed references to the abundant literature, of the matter by Prof. Brownlie in his famous international law textbook. In dealing with multinational corporations among the "controversial candidatures" for being subjects of international law, he rejects the proposal by some jurists with regard to concession agreements that

> "the relations of States and foreign corporations *as such* should be treated on the international plane and not as an aspect of the normal rules governing the position of aliens and their assets on the territory of a State. In principle, corporations of municipal law do not have international legal personality. Thus a concession or contract between a State and a foreign corporation is not governed by the law of treaties."[73]

Later, Professor Brownlie summarizes his detailed arguments against the various theories of internationalized contracts quite clearly as follows:

> "The rules of public international law accept the normal operation of rules of private international law and when a claim for a breach of contract between an alien and a government arises, the issue will be decided in accordance with the applicable system of municipal law designated by the rules of private international law. Further questions are raised if the parties to a State contract expressly choose an applicable law other than a particular system of local law,

---

tion treaties between the home State and the host State therefore offer more effective solutions.

70 For example, Kay Hailbronner, "Der Staat und der Einzelne as Völkerechtssubjekte", in Vitzthum (ed.), *Völkerrecht*, *op. cit.*, pp. 197-198.

71 Vol. 2, 1987, p. 214. A distinction is made between the internationalization of concession or development agreements and State contracts other than development agreements, pp. 213-216.

72 Ian Brownlie, *The Rule of Law in International Affairs*, 1998, ch. III., p. 35 *et seq.* Internationalized contracts are only very briefly mentioned at 149.

73 Brownlie, *Principles*, *op. cit.*, pp. 67-68.

> either 'general principles of law' or public international law. A choice by the parties of public international law is assumed by some writers to place the contract on the international plane, but this cannot be correct since a State contract is not a treaty and cannot involve State responsibility as an international obligation. In practice choice of law clauses in State contracts often specify the local law 'and such principles and rules of public international law as may be relevant', and in face of such clauses arbitrators have a certain discretion in selecting the precise role of public international law."[74]

It is submitted that this interpretation still reflects the current status of international law *de lege lata*. But there is a further point that needs to be taken into account. It is not conceivable that a host State could unilaterally elevate a private multinational company to a subject of international law with *erga omnes* effect. Such elevation would necessarily also affect the rights of the home State of the company,[75] whether this State is determined on the basis of the seat theory, the control theory or any other theory relevant to the difficult problem of the identification of the nationality of multinational companies.[76] Moreover, it would also indirectly affect the position of other States in the international legal system. Even if one would assume that the attribution of international legal personality (in a limited sense) could only have relative legal effect, namely vis-à-vis the host State concluding the contract, problems affecting the position of the home State in terms of its right to diplomatic protection of the multinational company may arise.[77]

It is also not in the public interest of States that multinational corporations, representing primarily private commercial interests of their owners, shareholders and managers, are legally placed on the level of international law as active subjects, making their national regulation and control more cumbersome than it already is. On the other hand, multinational companies also so far appear to be reluctant to claim a formal role within the system of international law. The costs of such a position may outweigh the benefits and it may be more convenient and effective to make use of informal mechanisms and economic power to further their objectives, while leaving official responsibility for public matters to States. At any rate, the issue of the proper qualification of "internationalized contracts" has lost much of its previous significance because most relevant contracts are now placed under the national legal system of the host State.[78]

---

74 *Ibid.*, pp. 550-551.

75 P. Malanczuk, *Akehurst's*, *op. cit.*, p. 102.

76 *Ibid.*, p. 267 with further references.

77 See generally Yoram Dinstein, "Diplomatic Protection of Companies under International Law", in Karel Wellens (ed.), *International Law: Theory and Practice: Essays in Honour of Eric Suy*, 1998, pp. 505-517, with further references.

78 See Muchlinski, *Multinational Enterprises*, *op. cit.*, p. 497, noting that a shift in bargaining power to the foreign investor may result in the provision of guarantees similar in their effect to stabilization clauses under the law of the host State.

THE ROLE OF MULTINATIONAL ENTERPRISES IN THE NEGOTIATION OF TREATIES

Apart from the specific context of so-called internationalized contracts, which – as we have seen – are not really international treaties, multinational companies appear to be notably absent from the arena of international treaty-making. One recent writer on the subject has remarked: "Like a school child sitting outside a teacher's office, the TNC has been told to wait quietly until the States' work of international law is done."[79]

Compared to the extensive lobbying of NGOs, for example in the field of human rights or environmental protection, on the international level of rule-making, it seems that multinational companies have been much less concerned with international treaty-making and exerting influence to achieve results corresponding to their economic interests, at least on the international level, as distinct from the national foreign policy level and the lobbying of governments.[80] As Razeen Sally has shown:

> "Whatever the nature of MNE action on trade policy, one thing is clear: firm preferences penetrate public policy channels mainly at the national level and, in the case of the EU, at the supranational level as well; but rarely at the multilateral level, as was shown by the conspicuous absence of effective corporate lobbying to advance market-opening arrangements in many of the negotiating areas of the Uruguay Round of the GATT. MNEs still do not take the relevant international organizations all that seriously and prefer to concentrate their political action in relations with home and host governments as well as with other *national* actors."[81]

However, this general statement needs to be qualified with regard to special areas and particular institutions, although there is little systematic research on the matter. Moreover, the process of economic globalization in the 1990s requires States in trade negotiations and multilateral rule-making to be more aware of the private sector and the relevant corporate histories of their major trading and investment partners and thus acquire adequate knowledge of the structure and activities of the relevant multinational enterprises.[82]

---

[79] Fleur Johns, "The Invisibility of the Transnational Corporation: An Analysis of International Law and Legal Theory" (1994) 19 *Melbourne University Law Review*, p. 902.

[80] As to the role of American companies, which have been quite active in this respect, see Graham K. Wilson, "Corporate Political Strategies" (1990) 20 *British Journal of Political Science*, pp. 281-288. For an analysis of the influence of multinational enterprises on national public policy choices see Razeen Sally, "Public Policy and the Janus Face of the Multinational Enterprise: National Embeddedness and International Production", in Philip Gummett (ed.), *Globalization and Public Policy*, 1996, pp. 64-82.

[81] Sally, *ibid*., p. 76.

[82] See Richard Higgott, "Beyond Embedded Liberalism: Governing the International Trade Regime in an Era of Economic Nationalism", in Philip Gummmett (ed.), *Globalization, op. cit*., pp. 18-45, at 35; Susan Strange, "States, Firms and Diplomacy" (1992) 68 *International Affairs*, pp. 1-15.

Within the International Labour Organization (ILO), for example, there is a long tradition of representatives of both industry and trade unions taking part in its rule-making, with the right to speak and vote independently of government representatives. Moreover, multinational corporations have been involved in one way or another in an advisory function in the treaty negotiations on the United Nations Law of the Sea Convention, the negotiations on the UN Code for Transnational Corporations, the GATT/WTO negotiations[83] and the variety of instruments adopted within the framework of the OECD. It is also remarkable that chemical companies have been engaged in the consultative process that resulted in the conclusion of the Chemical Weapons Convention in 1993 and that their direct engagement with governments is considered as being vital for the implementation of the Convention.[84]

It is further interesting to note that the 1992 Report of the UN Conference on Environment and Development (UNCED) contains a special chapter on "Strengthening the Role of Business and Industry".[85] The Report argues that "[b]usiness and industry, including transnational corporations, and their representative organizations should be full participants in the implementation and evaluation of activities related to Agenda 21".[86]

On the regional level, the role of lobbying of companies within the framework of the European Community legislative process has been highlighted, but apparently there is also not much research done in this area.[87] It is most likely that simi-

---

83 See Jonathan Charney, "Transnational Corporations and Developing Public International Law" (1983) *Duke Law Journal of International Law,* p. 748 *et seq.*; Peter T. Muchlinski, "'Global Bukowna' Examined: Viewing the Multinational Enterprise as a Transnational Law-making Community", in *op. cit.*, Teubner (ed.), *Global Law Without a State*, 1997, pp. 95-101.

84 See for details Johns, *op. cit.*, pp. 902-903, with particular reference to an initiative of Australia.

85 UN Doc. A/CONF.151/26 (Vol. III), 14 August 1992, ch. 30.

86 *Ibid.*, para. 30.1. On the results of the Rio Conference see P. Malanczuk, "'Sustainable Development' – Some Critical Thoughts in the Light of the Rio Conference", in K. Ginther, E. Denters and P. de Waart (eds.), *Sustainable Development and Good Governance*, 1995, pp. 23-53; Malanczuk, "Die Konferenz der Vereinten Nationen über Umwelt und Entwicklung (UNCED) und das internationale Umweltrecht" [The United Nations Conference on Environment and Development and International Environmental Law], in U.Beyerlin, M. Bothe, R. Hofmann and E.-U. Petersmann (eds.), *Recht zwischen Umbruch und Bewahrung, Völkerrecht – Staatsrecht – Europarecht, Festschrift für Rudolf Bernhardt,* 1995, pp. 985-1002.

87 See Andrew M. McLaughlin, Grant Jordan and William A. Maloney, "Corporate Lobbying in the European Community" (1993) 31 *Journal of Common Market Studies,* pp. 191-212; Wyn Grant, Alberto Martinelli and William Paterson, "Large Firms as Political Actors: A Comparative Analysis of the Chemical Industry in Britain, Italy and West Germany" (1989) 12 *West European Politics,* pp. 72-90; Sonia Mazey and Jeremy Richardson (eds.), *Lobbying in the European Community*, 1993; M.P.C.M. Van Schendelen (ed.), *National and Private EC Lobbying*, 1993; Jacqueline Nonon and Michel Clamen, *L'Europe et ses Couloirs. Lobbying et lobbyistes*, 1991; Andrew M. McLaughlin and Justin Greenwood,

lar activities occur with regard to other regional economic arrangements, such as NAFTA or others affecting the trade and investment interests of multinational operators, although the pressure is probably exercised more directly on and through the national government.[88] It is also clear that, for example, multinational companies concerned with the international protection of intellectual property rights find the appropriate channels to convey their views. Thus, it is well known that the reluctance of the United States to join the Biodiversity Convention was at least in part a reaction to pressure exercised by the American pharmaceutical companies interested in commercially exploiting genetic resources in other countries.

Another example is the alleged initiative of multinational companies to produce the draft of the Multilateral Agreement of Investment (MAI) negotiated within the framework of the OECD, which, however, officials of the OECD declare to be a myth produced by NGO's and other groups opposing "globalization" and the rise of the multinational corporation.[89] Clearly, however, there is a history of a number of failed attempts in the past on the part of international business-orientated lobbying groups to achieve the adoption of a multilateral convention to protect the rights of investors within the framework of the International Chamber of Commerce (ICC), the OECD and the European Economic Community. A by-product of these failures was then the widespread use of bilateral investment protection and promotion treaties that are instances of home State intervention on behalf of home-based multinational enterprises.[90]

It is not true, on the other hand, that in the field of environmental standards, for example, multinational enterprises generally oppose strong international regulation. A recent UN survey on corporate views to environmental issues has demonstrated that two-thirds of the companies interviewed expressed a strong preference for more international standards.[91] Nevertheless, there are, of course, strong pressure groups on particular issues, such as the Global Climate Coalition, the main US industry organization lobbying against the Kyoto Protocol to the Climate Change Treaty, aiming at the reduction of greenhouse gas emissions.[92]

"The Management of Interest Representation in the European Union" (1995) 33 *Journal of Common Market Studies*, pp. 143-156.

88 See, for example, Lorraine Eden and Maureen Appel Molot, "Insiders and Outsiders: Auto Industry Policy Choices in the NAFTA Debate", in Robert G. Cushing *et al.* (eds.), *The Challenge of NAFTA*, 1993, pp. 175-190.

89 On the draft MAI, see, for example, Biswajit Dhar and Sachin Chaturvedi, "Multilateral Agreement on Investment – An Analysis" (1998) 33 *Economic and Political Weekly*, pp. 837-848; Peter Muchlinski, "Towards a Multilateral Investment Agreement (MAI): The OECD and WTO Models and Sustainable Development", in Friedl Weiss, Erik Denters and Paul de Waart (eds.), *International Economic Law with a Human Face*, 1998, pp. 429-451.

90 See Peter T. Muchlinski, "Global Bukowina", *op. cit.*, pp. 93-95.

91 See Muchlinski, *ibid.*, at 446.

92 In 1999 Royal Dutch Shell, as British Petroleum one year earlier, decided to pull out of the Global Climate Coalition, *Financial Times* of 22 April 1999, p. 5.

Be that as it may, there are also indications that multinational corporations are becoming more aware of the necessity to engage more vocally in international negotiations and represent their interests also in the international treaty-making processes more directly. Mr. David de Pury, President of the Finanzgesellschaft de Pury Pictet Turrettini & Co. AG, Zürich, Genf, has stated the problem in a recent article on the delicate relationship between economics and politics under the conditions of globalization of the economy.[93] Generally speaking, the author pleads for improved co-operation between economic and political actors in addressing the need of building a more appropriate international order with global rules of the game. Among the considerations of the author directly relevant to the topic of this paper, the observation is most interesting that the problems of the international order is not a predominant issue, neither for companies, nor for governments.[94] As far as international companies are concerned, they operate within the existing international system (or non-system) as profitably as possible. Only few attempt to contribute to the required changes of the system. The private sector thus largely neglects the relevance of the international framework conditions. One of the conclusions is that economic actors need to organize themselves more efficiently on the international level and must engage in an active dialogue with States and international organizations. The author notes that there is a discrepancy between the dynamic process of global economic integration and the slow process of international negotiations between governments. As the private sector has an interest to exercise pressure to speed up the rhythm of this process, it needs to have ideas on the desirable international framework and "organisms".[95]

The problem here is that there are hundreds of national and international business associations dealing with the topic of the international framework conditions of their operations, few of which are seen as being effective. The author finds some light in the tunnel in the fact that Mr. Helmut Maucher, CEO of Nestlé and President of the International Chamber of Commerce (ICC), started a dialogue with the international institutions in Geneva, in particular with the WTO. He also suggests that the big companies in the financial sector should commence such a dialogue with the IMF and the World Bank in Washington. The aim of such dialogue is to disperse the perception that globalization primarily serves the interests of large capital and leads to the suppression of the economically weak.[96] A counter-offensive seems to be required.

In fact, this counter-offensive has already started and it may result in a more active role of multinational corporations in lobbying in international institutions and their law-making activities. This was the declared programme of Mr. Maucher

---

[93] David de Pury, "Wer regiert die Weltwirtschaft? – Das Spannungsverhältnis von Wirtschaft und Politik" (1998) 53 No. 11 *Internationale Politik,* pp. 25-30.

[94] *Ibid.*, p. 27.

[95] *Ibid.*, p. 29.

[96] *Ibid.*

when he became the new President of the ICC at the beginning of 1997.[97] In his view, globalization transfers more and more decisions to the level of international bodies which requires that industry and commerce take a more active international stand than previously, for example, on issues like trade, corruption or harmonization of competition rules. In fact, at a WTO Trade Facilitation Symposium, held from 9-10 March in Geneva, to discuss practical problems traders face when moving goods across borders, some of the world's leading corporations were represented.[98]

It is clear that this initiative is fermented by the activities of environment and human rights NGOs that have been presenting their views much more effectively than business on the international level. Criticism from "civil society" has also induced some multinational companies (i.e. Shell, British Petroleum, Rio Tinto) to commit themselves to human rights and/or the protection of the environment in internal corporate codes of conduct.[99]

On the other hand, it is notable that the United Nations itself is seeking to forge closer ties between the UN and private business. In 1998 a new partnership was inaugurated between the UN at its headquarters in New York with the International Chamber of Commerce. Among the 25 companies represented at the meeting were Alcatel Alsthom, BAT Industries, Coca Cola, McDonald's and Unilever.[100]

THE ROLE OF MULTINATIONAL ENTERPRISES IN THE IMPLEMENTATION OF TREATIES

As noted above, a specific role for multinational companies in the implementation of international instruments has been foreseen, for example, in the non-binding Agenda 21 of the Rio Conference on Environment and Development and in the context of the Chemical Weapons Convention. However, the implementation of treaties may also be secured by granting specific procedural rights to certain actors. Just as human rights treaties, under certain conditions, may grant not only benefits to individuals, but also rights in the sense of having legal standing in dispute settlement mechanisms and thereby a formal role in the implementation of the relevant treaties, certain treaties also may provide multinational companies with such a function. This may even be the case under international human rights guarantees, whenever they may be enjoyed also by a company (like the right to property).

Most international tribunals, however, are not open to individuals or companies; for instance, Article 34 of the Statute of the International Court of Justice

---

97 *Frankfurter Allgemeine Zeitung*, 12 February 1997, p. 15.

98 See the information provided by the WTO, 3 March 1998, http://www.wto.org/goods/trade_release.htm.

99 See *Financial Times,* 28 April 1998, p. 9; *NRC Handelsblad* of 26 May 1998, p. 16.

100 *Financial Times*, 17 March 1998, p. 5.

provides that only States may be parties to contentious cases before the Court.[101] But there are exceptions; thus, the International Bank for Reconstruction and Development (the World Bank) has set up an international arbitral tribunal to hear disputes arising out of investments between States and the nationals of other States (ICSID).[102] At the Iran-United States Claims Tribunal, individuals and companies, which are nationals of one of the two parties, have legal standing under certain conditions.[103] The procedure of the United Nations Compensation Commission (UNCC), set up by the UN Security Council in Geneva in 1991 after the defeat of Iraq in the Second Gulf War, even attempts to give priority to the masses of claims of individual victims rather than to the claims of big companies against Iraq (it is not, however, really operating as an arbitral or judicial body).[104] The Permanent Court of Arbitration (PCA) in The Hague in 1993 modified its procedure to encourage access of "Parties of which only one is a State".[105] Under the 1988 Canada-United States Free Trade Agreement (FTA),[106] private parties have access to binational panels which can reach binding decisions in certain cases.[107] The procedure has also been made part of the North American Free Trade Agreement (NAFTA).[108] On the other hand, proposals to grant private parties which are directly affected by alleged breaches of GATT rules access to the GATT dispute settlement system,[109] in order to relieve them from the discretion of their home

---

101 For criticism of this limitation see E. Lauterpacht, *Aspects of the Administration of International Justice*, 1991.

102 See Malanczuk, *Akehurst's*, *op. cit.*, pp. 295-296; Muchlinski, *Multinational Enterprises*, *op. cit.*, p. 540 *et seq.*; Christoph Schreuer, "Access to ICSID Dispute Settlement for Locally Incorporated Companies", in Weiss, Denters and Waart (eds.), *International Economic Law, op. cit.*, pp. 497-512; Schreuer, "The Interpretation of ICSID Arbitration Agreements", in Karel Wellens (ed.), *International Law*, *op. cit.*, pp. 719-735.

103 See Malanczuk, *Akehurst's*, pp. 296-8; Malanczuk, "The Iran-United States Claims Tribunal in The Hague – Some Reflections on a Unique Institution of International Dispute Settlement Moving towards the End of its Work", in V. Götz, P. Selmer and R. Wolfrum (eds.), *Liber Amicorum Günther Jaenicke – zum 85 Geburtstag*, 1998, pp. 221-238.

104 See P. Malanczuk, "International Business and New Rules of State Responsibility? – The Law Applied by the United Nations (Security Council) Compensation Commission for Claims against Iraq", in K.-H. Böckstiegel (ed.), *Perspectives of Air Law, Space Law and International Business Law for the Next Century, Proceedings of an International Colloquium, Cologne, June 7-9, 1995 to Celebrate 70 Years Institute of Air and Space Law and 20 Years Chair for International Business Law of the University of Cologne*, 1996, pp. 117-45; Malanczuk, *Akehurst's*, pp. 398-399 with further references.

105 See Malanczuk, *Akehurst's*, p. 294.

106 See Malanczuk, *Akehurst's*, pp. 225 and 300.

107 For example, in disputes concerning investment, anti-dumping and countervailing measures (Article 1904 FTA). See J.-G. Castel, "The Settlement of Disputes under the 1988 Canada-United States Free Trade Agreement" (1989) 83 *American Journal of International Law*, pp. 118-128.

108 See Malanczuk, *Akehurst's*, pp. 225 and 300.

109 See Malanczuk, *Akehurst's*, pp. 233 and 300; Marcel Brus, *Third Party Dispute Settlement in an Interdependent World*, 1995, pp. 207-208 with references. Debra P. Steger,

governments to take up the complaint, have not been included in the reform of the dispute settlement mechanism under the WTO arrangements.[110] (The discussion, to which extent municipal law could be used to grant individuals and companies access to international trade dispute settlement (via the possible direct effect of WTO agreements in national law), is a complicated matter beyond the scope of this presentation.)[111] Similarly, in the European Communities individuals and companies can bring claims before the Court of Justice of the European Communities, although it must be pointed out that the supranational structure of the European Community makes it a unique case in international law.

Some authors argue that transnational corporations have obtained a "limited, functional international personality" through procedures such as under ICSID, the Law of the Sea Convention's provisions relating to the settlement of deep sea-bed mining disputes or under the World Bank Convention establishing the Multilateral Investment Guarantee Agency (MIGA).[112] But it is admitted that this status is conditional because it depends on the prior consent of the home State of the company to be bound by the respective treaties, and as far as the Law of the Sea Convention is concerned upon State sponsorship of the relevant company.[113]

It is further important to note that in bilateral investment treaties concluded between States the recent trend has been to move towards supplying the private investor with a direct and compulsory right to invoke international arbitration procedures against the host State, although the doctrinal basis of this right is not quite clear in the literature.[114] As noted by Waelde,

> "Though these new methods still sail under the flag of 'dispute settlement', they need to be understood less as a part of the traditional instrument of

---

"WTO Dispute Settlement: Revitalization of Multilateralism After the Uruguay Round" (1996) 9 *Leiden Journal of International Law,* pp. 319-335; Friedl Weiss, "Third Parties in GATT/WTO Dispute Settlement Proceedings", in Denters and Schrijver (eds.), *Reflections*, *op. cit.*, pp. 458-472.

110 For a brief survey see Brus, *op. cit.,* pp. 28-37. For a recent reconsideration of the matter see Panel discussion, "Is the WTO Dispute Settlement Mechanism Responsive to the Needs of the Traders? Would a System of Direct Action by Private Parties Yield Better Results?" (1998) 32 *Journal of World Trade Law,* pp. 147-165.

111 See Berned-Roland Killmann, "The Access of Individuals to International Trade Dispute Settlement" (1996) 13 *Journal of International Arbitration,* pp. 143-169.; Michael A. Geist, "Toward a General Agreement on the Regulation of Foreign Direct Investment" (1995) 26 *Law and Policy in International Business,* pp. 673-669.

112 D. Kokkini-Iatridou and P.J.I.M. de Waart, *Legal Personality*, *op. cit.*, at 117-124; 129-131; D. Kokkini-Iatridou and P.J.I.M de Waart, "Economic Disputes Between States and Private Parties: Some Legal Thoughts on the Institutionalization of Their Settlement" (1986) 33 *Netherlands International Law Review,* pp. 289-333, at 323-325; Nico Schrijver, *Sovereignty over Natural Resources. Balancing Rights and Duties*, 1997, pp. 7-8.

113 Schrijver, *ibid.*, p. 8.

114 See Thomas W. Waelde, "Investment Arbitration Under the Energy Charter Treaty – From Dispute Settlement to Treaty Implementation" (1996) 12 *Arbitration International,* p. 429 *et seq.*, at 434-436.

> "Though these new methods still sail under the flag of 'dispute settlement', they need to be understood less as a part of the traditional instrument of providing contractual arbitration to settle disputes arising out of the parties' relationship in lieu of courts, but rather as an instrument of enhancing treaty compliance using private agents motivated by and resourced with commercial interest. There is nothing particularly new about using private agents to enforce law; ... most areas of economic law relay to a large extent on individuals and companies litigating against infringements. What is new is that this key instrument of achieving compliance is employed in international law and against States. It signifies a conspicuous climb-down of States – i.e. government bureaucracies – from their superior position of sovereignty when confronting private litigants on the equal level of an arbitral tribunal."[115]

It is important to consider, however, that this mainly applies to treaties concluded with developing countries and countries that emerged from the break-up of the Soviet Union. The main industrialized countries (including the USA, Norway and continental Europe) have excluded disputes arising from their oil and gas contracts from recourse to international arbitration, although on the international level they have always been opposing the Calvo-doctrine advanced by Latin American countries.[116]

The 1995 Energy Charter Treaty (Art. 26) has further developed the forms of providing for the access of private investors to international arbitration with damage claims against States without having to conduct specific negotiations on individual investment protection clauses. Under the Treaty there is no corresponding right of the host State against the private investor. Indeed, this may have far-reaching implications, affecting also the contract bargaining between governments and foreign companies in the light of the Treaty and its dispute settlement mechanisms.[117]

Finally, the OECD draft on the Multilateral Agreement on Investment (MAI) should be mentioned. As in the case of the Energy Charter Treaty, there are two types of dispute settlement mechanisms included in the draft MAI: State-State disputes and investor-State disputes. In the latter case the investor can directly invoke arbitration against their host States in cases of alleged breach of the MAI. However, there is disagreement on the proper scope of the relevant provision in a number of important details.[118] At the time of writing, the OECD negotiations on the MAI were shelved, due to disagreement among the parties, and there is also resis-

---

115 Waelde, *ibid.*, at 437.

116 Waelde, *ibid.*

117 See further Thomas W. Waelde, "Sustainable Development and the 1994 Energy Charter Treaty: Between Pseudo-Action and the Management of Environmental Investment Risk", in Weiss, Denters and Waart (eds.), *International Economic Law* , *op. cit.*, pp. 223-270.

118 See Ambassador Marino Baldi, "Dispute Settlement", *Symposium on the MAI, 20 October 1997, Cairo, Egypt*, http://www.oecd.org/daf/cmis/mai/baldi4.htm

tance from developing countries to placing the issue of a multilateral framework for investment on the WTO agenda.[119]

The position granted to companies under such investor-State dispute settlement mechanisms is not without problems, as can be seen from the experience under the NAFTA agreement. In 1998 Canada had to pay US$ 13 million to the Ethyl corporation of the United States for a claim against Canada's ban on the use of MMT, a petrol additive, and agreed to lift the ban despite objections from environmental groups and the motor vehicle industry, which alleges that MMT interferes with emission control systems. Another claim against Canada has been filed by the US company SD Myers which deals in cleaning up polychlorinated biphenyls (PCB) waste. The company seeks damages over Canada's ban, imposed in 1995, on the export of PCB waste on the basis of business allegedly lost worth millions of dollars. Canada is now looking for interpretative changes to the NAFTA agreement to restrict the ability of private companies to claim compensation for government regulations that harm their business.[120] The concern is that the investor-State arbitration provision is being extended to prevent governments from enacting legitimate regulations. Environmental groups voiced similar criticism against the draft Multilateral Agreement on Investment (MAI).

Conclusions

Within the limited framework of this paper, only a general survey of some important aspects of the role of multinational enterprises in treaty-making could be provided. Nevertheless, the following conclusions may be drawn:

a) Multinational companies are still formally not "subjects of international law" in any meaningful sense of the term, although there is limited recognition of their legal personality in certain dispute settlement mechanisms. As such, their existence is barely recognized by general international law (in contrast to a few number of special soft law instruments aiming at the regulation of their activities).
b) They are not parties to multilateral and bilateral treaties in the sense of international law; so-called State contracts or "internationalized contracts" are not treaties in the sense of international law and cannot elevate them to "partial subjects of international law".
c) Multinational enterprises have a formal consultative or informal lobbying function in the negotiation of certain types of treaties relevant to their commercial activities. It is likely that this role will be expanded in the fu-

---

119 See, for example, B.B. Ramaiah, "Towards a multilateral framework on investment?" (1997) 6 *Transnational Corporations,* pp. 117-121; P. Malanczuk, "State-State and Investor-State Dispute Settlement in the OECD Draft Multilateral Agreement on Investment" [forthcoming] (2000) 3 *Journal of International Economic Law.*

120 *Financial Times*, 22 January 1999, p. 15.

ture, also in view of the current trend in the United Nations to seek stronger co-operation with the private business sector.

d) Multinational companies are increasingly achieving a stronger independent role in implementing treaties relevant to their activities (i.e. foreign investment) vis-à-vis host States through their legal standing and rights in dispute settlement mechanisms under the particular bilateral or multilateral treaty (or draft treaty). In this limited sense they are attaining international legal personality, derivative, however, from the respective treaty and granted by States under a public international agreement. Such rights are conditional on the consent of States. Moreover, rights granted by treaty can also be revoked by treaty amendment or they may expire by lawful termination of the treaty.

Especially the last conclusion reminds one of the proposition " Where there are rights, there also should be duties". A recent study on the multilateral investment system and multinational enterprises by Brewer and Young concludes:

> "The philosophy of interments has swung markedly away from the obligations of firms and rights of governments to firms' rights and governments' obligations. This is a reflection of the changing attitudes and priorities at the host country level and the recognition of the beneficial contribution of international investment. For future negotiations, it would be unrealistic to ignore issues concerning the obligations of firms, given the bargaining power of MNEs and the distributional implications of their actions, especially in developing countries. The next decade may thus see a substantial change in the nature of MNE/government relations."[121]

A related question is whether it is possible and desirable under international law (*de lege ferenda*) to establish direct liability of multinational companies, at least for violations of certain fundamental norms of international law. As mentioned above, some recent cases filed in the United States have given rise to a discussion of this matter.[122] In theory, such liability could also be conceived as a form of treaty implementation, where such norms are not only customary, but are also embodied in treaties, i.e. the prohibition of slavery or torture. But this is a complex topic which needs to be discussed at a separate occasion.

---

121 Brewer and Young, *The Multilateral Investment System*, *op. cit.*, p. 273.

122 See M. Kamminga and S. Zia-Zarifi (eds.), *Corporate Liability*, *op. cit.* n. 2.

Luncheon Address

Chair: ROBERT ROSENSTOCK

CHARLES N. BROWER[*]

The International Treaty-Making Process: Paradise Lost, or Humpty Dumpty?

The question I have sought to pose – though I confess a much easier familiarity with Mother Goose's *oeuvre* than with John Milton's baroque extravaganza – is whether the international treaty-making system as we have known it is forever gone, irretrievably shattered, beyond the reach of reconstructive surgery, or whether instead its demise represents, like the biblical loss of innocence, an event which, while of the most fundamental significance, is, in the end, one element in an endless struggle between eternally contending forces.

But perhaps I should elaborate my premise before going further: It is that the public international law treaty-making process has become so fraught with contentiousness as to be virtually a non-starter for many important causes.

Let me begin with the egregious example of the United Nations global warming conference attended in Kyoto in December 1997 by 159 delegations. The United States delegation included the Vice President of the United States, whose arrival at the eleventh hour was understood to be a confirmation that the United States intended to participate in an agreement. That summit also was attended, however, by several United States Senators, members of the legislative body which under the United States Constitution must give its advice and consent by a two-thirds majority before the President can ratify international treaties negotiated by the Executive Branch. Those Senators publicly expressed varying, and, in some cases, inconsistent, opinions on the subject of the summit and the United States' participation in it. In the end, after highly contentious negotiations – so exhausting that at a critical point interpreters reportedly walked off the job – delegates reached a partial agreement that was described in the American press as "moderate" while postponing decisions on more difficult matters until later this year. Even before seeing the final text of that partial agreement, however, leading members of the United States Senate denounced it publicly, declaring it was "dead on arrival."[1]

The Kyoto example, while uniquely graphic, is not an isolated incident. Earlier in 1997, the United States Senate barely approved the Chemical Weapons

* I would like to thank Anne D. Smith, Counsel, White & Case LLP, for her assistance in the preparation of this address.

1 *The Washington Post*, 11 December, 1997, p. A37.

V. Gowlland-Debbas (ed.), Multilateral Treaty-making, 75–80.

Convention[2] after a legislative roller coaster ride. Under a Republican Administration the United States Government had been a leading proponent of the Convention. Under a Democratic Administration the United States Government continued to view it as important to national security. Nonetheless, when it became clear that Senate approval was unlikely, the Senate vote on the Convention was postponed from a date before the 1996 Presidential election to a date after the election, which latter date was only a few days before the treaty in fact entered into force. On that latter date advice and consent to ratification was wrung from a Republican-dominated Senate only after a significant fight that raised the spectre that a country that had led the fight to reach agreement on a treaty of great international importance might nonetheless fail to ratify it because of intervening partisan domestic issues.

Unfortunately, what I am describing is by no means a new situation, or one that applies only to macro-political issues. As long ago as 1969 the United States played a leading role in negotiation of the Vienna Convention on the Law of Treaties at a conference of more than 100 nations. It signed that Convention, along with almost 50 other countries, on 23 May, 1969.[3] Although the Convention was submitted to the United States Senate for its advice and consent in 1971, that body has never acted on it, due to asserted concerns about the effect of ratification on domestic constitutional issues. Nonetheless, notwithstanding the lack of ratification – or perhaps because of it – the United States Government has been compelled expressly to recognise that the Convention largely restates customary international law that the United States accepts,[4] and courts in the United States apply the rules of the Vienna Convention as customary international law.[5] Similarly, although objections to the provisions originally agreed in the 1982 United Nations Convention on the Law of the Sea that address deep sea mining prevented ratification of that treaty by the United States and some other countries, the United States nonetheless has accepted virtually the balance of the Convention as customary international law binding on all States.[6] This device of applying the terms of unratified treaties as customary law has inherent limits, of course, and can hardly be regarded as a solution.

---

2 Convention on the Prohibition of Development, Production, Stockpiling and Use of Chemical Weapons and on Their Destruction, opened for signature 13 January, 1993, S. Treaty Doc. 103-21, (1996) 32 ILM, p. 800 [hereinafter Chemical Weapons Convention].

3 Vienna Convention on the Law of Treaties, 23 May, 1969, 1155 UNTS 331 (entered into force 27 January, 1980) [hereinafter Vienna Convention].

4 See *U.S. v. Iran*, December 37-A17-FT (13 May, 1985), reprinted in 8 Iran – U.S. Cl. Trib. Rep. 189, 207 (1985) (Vienna Convention treated by authorities in the United States as statement of customary international law).

5 See, *e.g.*, *Kreimerman v. Casa Veerkamp, A.S. de C.V.*, 22 F.3d 634, 638 (5th Cir.), cert. denied, 115 S. Ct. 577 (1994); *Day v. Trans World Airlines, Inc.*, 528 F.2d 21, 33 (2d Cir. 1975), cert.denied, 429 U.S. 890 (1976).

6 United Nations Convention on the Law of the Sea, 10 December, 1982, UN Doc. A/CONF. 62/122 (entered into force 16 November, 1994).

While I have dwelt just now on the record of my own country, I hasten to note that it is not alone in this regard. Other countries have similar difficulties. For example, due to inability to achieve agreement among its provinces, Canada has never joined the convention establishing the International Centre for the Settlement of Investment Disputes at the World Bank, a self-contained and widely accepted regime for deciding investment disputes.[7] And for months after the United States succeeded in ratifying the Chemical Weapons Convention last year, significant doubt persisted as to the participation in the Convention by Russia, holder of one of the world's largest chemical weapons stockpiles, due to political concerns in the Duma over the expense of complying with treaty provisions.

Why are we in such a mess? There are at least five causes:

1) The proliferation of players, i.e. nation-States. The United Nations, at its founding on 24 October, 1945, had 27 members. Today it has 185, a nearly sevenfold increase.[8] This is reflected in the mushrooming number of parties to treaties. In 1947, for example, the Convention on International Civil Aviation ("Chicago Convention") came into force after ratification by only 26 States.[9] Now the number of ratifying States is 185, more than seven times the original number of parties.[10]
2) The growth of democracy within this greatly expanded community of nations. Just look, for example, at the 26 States whose ratifications of that same Chicago Convention brought it into force more than 50 years ago, on 4 April, 1947. Roughly two-thirds of them could have been described as democracies at the time; now all but one of them qualify. The political cacophony that inevitably arises in a community of close to 200 predominantly democratic States is not designed to promote efficiency in international law-making.
3) The post-Cold War spread of strife among ethnic, regional, tribal, religious, and other groupings within States or across State boundaries. The domestic political pressures that result from such turmoil inevitably preoccupy the affected national governments and often weaken or restrict their ability to act decisively in international affairs.
4) What Professor Steven R. Ratner in a recent article in the magazine *Foreign Policy* termed "this century's great trend in international law: the increasing international regulation of more and more issues once typically

---

[7] Convention on the Settlement of Investment Disputes between States and Other States, 18 March, 1965, 17 UST1270, 575 UNTS 159.

[8] United Nations Member States (last modified 17 July, 1997) http://www.un.org/Overview/unmember.html

[9] Convention on International Civil Aviation, 7 December, 1944, 61 Stat. 1180, 15 UNTS 295 (entered into force 4 April, 1947).

[10] [October 1997] ICAO Journal at 30.

seen as part of State domestic jurisdiction", including "new domains from the environment to the Internet".[11]

5) The rise of non-governmental organizations ("NGOs") and other non-State actors as influential participants in the public international law-making process. Their role in Kyoto was enormous, and NGO coalitions in recent years effectively have caused the International Court of Justice to rule on the lawfulness of nuclear weapons,[12] and have been instrumental in the movement to create a standing International Criminal Court. Such "single issue" organizations' single-minded pursuit of their goals increasingly has an impact on international treaty negotiations. Moreover, the trend just cited, *i.e.*, to subject to international regulation more and more subjects previously regarded as of purely domestic relevance, brings the affected interests onto the stage just as assuredly as does any domestic legislative process.

To assess the impact on the treaty-making process of at least some of these five factors one need only look at the issue of air carrier liability to passengers and for cargo.

For more than 40 years, the issue of liability limits under the 1929 Warsaw Convention has been a matter of increasing debate, frequent negotiation and occasional agreement. Yet the many attempts to amend that treaty in this respect have been notably unsuccessful.[13] In 1971, the Guatemala City Protocol was negotiated and it still is not in force. The subsequently negotiated Montreal Protocols Nos. 3 and 4 similarly have remained in limbo. Aside from the Hague Protocol of 1955,[14] which, incidentally, the United States did not ratify, the only effective post-Warsaw agreements on liability limitations have been privately agreed contractual ones: The Montreal Interim Agreement in 1966[15] and the IATA Inter-Carrier Agreement on Passenger Liability and Implementation Agreement. Indeed, no significant multilateral treaty on any aspect of aviation has been concluded and actually entered

---

11 Steven R. Ratner, "International Law: The Trials of Global Norms", [Spring 1998] *Foreign Policy,* at 65-67.

12 Legality of the Threat or Use of Nuclear Weapons (Request for Advisory Opinion by the General Assembly of the United Nations), UN Doc. A/51/218/Oct. 15, 1996, (1996) 35 ILM, p. 809.

13 Protocol to Amend the Warsaw Convention, 8 March, 1971, 10 ILM p. 613 [hereinafter Guatemala City Protocol] still is not in force; Protocols to Amend the Warsaw Convention, 25 September, 1975, S. Exec. Doc. No. 1, 98th Cong., 1st Sess. 23-36 (1983), reprinted in 22 ILM, p. 13, [hereinafter Montreal Protocols Nos. 3 and 4] also are not in force.

14 Protocol to Amend the Convention for the Unification of Certain Rules Relating to International Carriage by Air, 28 September, 1955, 478 UNTS 371 (1967).

15 Agreement Relating to Liability Limitations of Warsaw Convention and the Hague Protocol, 13 May, 1966, Agreement C.A.B. 18990 (approved by order E-23680).

into force in the last 25 years, that is since the entry into force on 26 January, 1973, of the Montreal Sabotage Convention.[16]

Well? Accepting my premise, which I think is inescapable, what can be done?

The advice I have given the international air carriers, and would give private industry in general, is to privatize the international law-making process to the maximum extent possible. These days almost anything can be privatized. Such things as army mess halls and even jails now are operated by profit-seeking entrepreneurs, a previously unthinkable state of affairs. International law-making for industry also can be privatized to a very large degree, as the international air carriers, for example, are doing.

A second route is, as indicated, more elaboration of custom. As earlier noted, conventions to which one or another major power does not become a party nevertheless sometimes can be brought to bind that State as custom. The development of purely customary law may be encouraged as well, as we have seen, for example, in the fairly harmonious rules that have emerged in various States on the subject of sovereign immunity. They, in fact, provide a good example of the effective implementation of international law by municipal court systems.

There are however, limits to the possibilities of these alternatives. Some attachment to the power of States inevitably will be required in order to secure enforcement of private contractual undertakings if and when they are not honoured. Custom has the disadvantage of being evolutionary, hence often uncertain, disputed, and therefore contentious. In the end, an inter-State legislative process that functions is indispensable.

But how can we secure it? That, of course, is why we are here today. One answer given has been to favour, wherever practicable, so-called "framework" conventions which establish broad obligations but permit gradual compliance through national adjustment of norms without further resort to the ratification process. Another is to remit the international legislative process to specialized, sectoral bodies, and to regional organizations, which may be best able to fashion conventions that in fact will clear municipal ratification hurdles. A further response has been to encourage the development of soft law, the progressive reshaping and modification of which may provide a sound basis for the adoption of viable hard-law conventions. Other solutions have been touched on during this Forum.

And now, to return to my theme: Can we regroup, or is all lost? Are we dealing with Paradise Lost, or with Humpty-Dumpty?

In researching my subject, I learned, much to my surprise, that at least according to one interpretation, Humpty-Dumpty, paralleling Milton's great poem up

---

16 Convention for the Suppression of Unlawful Acts Against the Safety of Civil Aviation, 23 September, 1971, 24 UST 564 (entered into force 26 January, 1973) [hereinafter Montreal Sabotage Convention]. A supplementary Protocol applying it also to airports entered into force 6 August, 1989. Protocol for the Suppression of Unlawful Acts of Violence at Airports Serving Civil Aviation, 24 February, 1988, S. Treaty Doc. 100-19, (1988) 27 ILM, p. 627 (entered into force 6 August, 1989).

to a point, itself "presents a vivid metaphor for the Fall of Man and subsequent biblical events".[17] That interpretation continues:

> However, in Revelations at least a few pure and rejecting of sin are allowed to dwell in the final glory of God's Kingdom on earth. Humpty-Dumpty, in many ways one of the most troubling works of modern literature, despairs even this hope.[18]

I, however, do not entertain despair. I find it incompatible with what I regard as the implicitly optimistic concept of the rule of law. I believe instead that although the international legislative process, as we have known it, is no more, it is being, and inevitably must be, supplanted by a new one.

It is our duty to apply ourselves to this task. Today is a good beginning.

---

[17] Northwestern University (last modified 24 September, 1996) <http://pubweb.nwu.edu/~jww990/humpty.html> .

[18] *Id.*

Multilateral Treaties and the Collective Interest

Chair: STEPHEN McCAFFREY

BRUNO SIMMA

How Distinctive Are Treaties Representing Collective Interest? The Case of Human Rights Treaties

The purpose of this presentation is to briefly analyze the distinctive features of human rights treaties with regard to: formation; the nature of obligations created; interpretation; reservations; denunciation; and State succession.

FORMATION

The role of international organizations – and of the United Nations in particular – has been particularly intensive in human rights treaty-making. At the universal level, there is now a distinctive and regular pattern of human rights law-formation: that is, to a much greater extent than is the case in environmental law and some other fields, it is through the relevant United Nations bodies that most, if not all, universal human rights instruments are elaborated. In fact the UN Commission on Human Rights could well be said to have a quasi-monopoly in this area. The role of non-governmental organizations has been discussed earlier by Professor Doswald-Beck. I would differ from her view only in saying that greater recognition of their significance might be justified as far as the negotiation phase is concerned.

The impact of "soft law" on the formation of human rights treaties is equally noteworthy. Today, the way towards a human rights treaty is paved by a series of soft law stages. It is almost a rule in contemporary human rights law-making that, at one stage or another, the UN Commission on Human Rights would adopt a declaration on a given subject area, e.g. the rights of the child or prohibition of torture, which would then be "hardened" into a full-fledged treaty. In this regard, the French expression "pre-droit" is very much to the point.

The words "soft law," to be sure, have another – and negative – connotation, namely that of "softness" of obligations, as pointed out by Professor Boyle and Mr. Johnson. However, there is nothing "soft" about progressive obligations, such as a State's obligation to undertake steps "to the maximum of its available resources, with a view to achieving progressively the full realization of the rights … ", as expressed in the International Covenant on Economic, Social and Cultural Rights (Article 2(1)). Surely, these obligations are more difficult to apply in practice, and performance of such obligations by States parties will be more difficult to assess

V. Gowlland-Debbas (ed.), Multilateral Treaty-making, 83–87.

legally, but still they cannot be regarded less "hard" as treaty obligations simply because of the way in which they are formulated.

THE NATURE OF OBLIGATIONS

At the regional level – most notably in the European context – human rights obligations undertaken among States by concluding a treaty have been metamorphosing into a set of objective laws. The European Court and the European Commission of Human Rights have been particularly vocal in advocating the position that, over and above contractual obligations, the European Convention on Human Rights has established a "public order" (*ordre public*) in Europe, and that the Convention forms part of a Constitution of Europe placed under a collective guarantee.

To what extent, if at all, is the "European" image of human rights law as a higher law transferable to the United Nations? It seems that, in order for the metamorphosis to occur at the universal level, there must be, in addition to the substantive law, a viable judicial control with institutions empowered to make binding decisions. In Europe, at least, both the European Convention on Human Rights and European Community law have just such organs – the European Court of Human Rights and the Court of Justice of the European Communities, respectively – capable of extracting States' compliance even with decisions that are extremely painful for them. Through such jurisprudence as well as institutional and procedural developments, what the founding members considered as treaties – and hence instruments contractual in nature – are being transformed into a more "constitutional" system. The question of transferability of the Strasbourg regime on reservations to human rights treaties will be discussed later in greater detail.

INTERPRETATION

Generally speaking, human rights treaty interpretation is characterized by the "teleological" approach. In the European context, however, the Strasbourg court has taken the matter one step further by adopting what it calls a "dynamic" or "evolutionary" method of interpretation. In the case of *Marckx v. Belgium* for example, the Court held that the European Convention on Human Rights is a "living instrument" that moves ahead and, in some respects, overtakes, as it were, the domestic law and the political intention of States. Such an interpretation, applied by powerful organs with binding authority such as the European Court of Human Rights, carries with it far-reaching and often painful consequences for States – so much so that several member governments of the European Convention or domestic supreme courts alluded at one stage to the possibility of leaving the Convention.

This experience is not confined to the European Convention. According to available information, the Netherlands, one of the most vocal human rights protagonists, came close to denouncing the International Covenant on Civil and Political Rights in 1988 because the Human Rights Committee adopted a similarly progressive interpretative approach to Art. 26 of the Covenant.

RESERVATIONS

The issue of reservations to human rights treaties has been a subject of active debate for several years. And it is justly so in light of the fact that, due to the distinctive character of human rights treaties, reservations entered by States parties play a particularly important role – quantitatively as well as qualitatively – in determining their rights and obligations arising from these treaties. Generally, reservations made to a treaty concern what States do *vis-à-vis* one another. As far as human rights treaties are concerned, however, reservations, which may be best described as "inward"-targeted, touch the heart of matters such as established legal practices or traditions within countries (for example, in the case of Austria, a Kelsenian tradition built into its constitution was found to be no longer compatible with the European Convention on Human Rights).

It is therefore essential that reservations be given a proper place with regard to human rights treaties. On the other hand, the question is how international law should deal with those reservations – made in a great number – which are clearly unacceptable. I am of the view that the Vienna Convention on the Law of Treaties is ill-equipped to fully address the specific challenge posed by human rights treaty reservations. Once again, in the European context, the Strasbourg court has developed a practice whereby it would first consider the admissibility of a particular reservation, and then proceed to sever reservations it finds inadmissible. At the universal level, a similar – but less successful – attempt was made by the Human Rights Committee. Its General Comment No. 24(52), in which the committee sought to defend the doctrine of severability, drew strong opposition from several major Western powers such as France, the United Kingdom and the United States, as well as the International Law Commission.

The discrepancy between the (lack of a) response of France and the United Kingdom to the Strasbourg court on the one hand, and that of the same States to the Human Rights Committee on the other, is striking. But are human rights treaties at the United Nations level structurally different from the European Convention so as to justify this discrepancy?

There is a growing practice of States – the Nordic countries prominent among them – according to which reservations regarded by objecting States as inadmissible are indeed severed. Typically, those States objecting to a reservation would make a declaration that they consider the reservation inadmissible and the reserving State as bound by the treaty in its entirety. Austria is also included in this group, though its position *vis-à-vis* the reservation concerned is usually more provisional or "procedure-oriented". Therefore, to state that the severability doctrine is impossible to implement in practice is without foundation. This doctrine could be brought in line with the principle of consent governing the formation of treaties by assuming that a State undertaking to ratify a human rights treaty with reservations takes the risk that, should the reservation in question be found inadmissible, it will be held to the treaty without the benefit of the unsuccessful reservation. If the reserving State finds this unacceptable, it might itself stay out of the treaty or be blocked by other States parties.

DENUNCIATION

Is there an "exit option" in case of human rights treaties? This question has gained currency in the human rights debate since the summer of 1997, when North Korea announced that it would leave the International Covenant on Civil and Political Rights. In response, the Office of the Legal Counsel of the United Nations expressed the view – supported by the human rights community – that the matter should be settled by reference to Article 56 of the Vienna Convention on the Law of Treaties. According to that article, if a treaty contains no provision on termination or does not provide for denunciation or withdrawal, it is "not subject to denunciation or withdrawal unless: (a) it is established that the parties intended to admit the possibility of denunciation or withdrawal; or (b) a right of denunciation or withdrawal may be implied by the nature of the treaty." On the basis that whereas the Covenant itself does not have any denunciation clause, its first Optional Protocol provides for denunciation (Article 12), as does the International Convention on the Elimination of all Forms of Racial Discrimination (Article 21), the Office considered that, in the case of the Covenant, the possibility of denunciation was not intended.

This argumentation, however, is not entirely satisfactory. I submit that from the same observation one may arrive at the exactly opposite conclusion. Take, for example, the question of fire in consular and diplomatic premises: Provisions on this matter are found in the 1963 Vienna Convention on Consular Relations but *not* in the Convention on Diplomatic Relations adopted two years earlier. Should this be understood as indicating that the parties did not intend to admit the possibility of the host State entering diplomatic (in contrast to consular) premises even if the mission is set afire, if a permission by its head is not given? The standard solution proposed in most textbooks is to say that in this case recourse to analogy is legitimate. But, then, there is no reason why an alleged lack of intention *a contrario* should be decisive in the case of the Civil and Political Covenant, on the sole basis that it contains no provision for denunciation.

To return to our question: Are human rights treaties subject to denunciation? Legally, any good lawyer would be able to argue in either direction. The present author, however, wishes to submit a policy argument in favour of an exit option for human rights treaties. It is clear that by ratifying a human rights treaty, States *volunteer* to assume obligations for the benefit of the human beings which the treaty seeks to protect; and, at least in the context of the United Nations, States cannot be coerced into obeying the obligations they have undertaken. Marriage, to take an analogous example, would probably not be viable as an institution any more should there be no possibility for divorce. The human rights régime should operate in a similar manner. Would the current drive by the United Nations towards the universality of human rights not be marked by contradiction if, on the one hand, the General Assembly encouraged States to adhere to the human rights treaties elaborated under its auspices, while on the other hand, the same Organization insisted that once in, States could not exit at a later stage?

For this reason, it is doubtful whether universality *qua* prescription of legal straitjacket would work. Further, the United Nations' uncompromising stance on denunciation might affect future State practice with respect to reservations: the less such denunciation is feasible the more the "quality" and quantity of reservations will increase.

STATE SUCCESSION

Since 1989, certain human rights advocates have interpreted State practice – i.e., patterns pursued by the successor States of the former Soviet Union or Yugoslavia – to the effect that there is now a rule of customary international law *in force* – not merely *emerging* – in support of automatic succession to human rights treaties. Such a principle of continuity of human rights treaty obligations was applied by the UN Human Rights Committee to Hong Kong after its transfer to the People's Republic of China.

However, a closer look at the relevant practice of States casts serious doubts about the principle's alleged customary status. Hence, the Committee on Economic, Social and Cultural Rights was right in taking a more guarded view when it issued a statement on the legal effects of the Economic and Social Covenant on Hong Kong. It is not clear, to say the least, whether the various actions and declarations of successor States can be seen as confirmations of continuity or declarations of accession. Their behaviour in apparent conformity with the principle of automatic succession, or continuity, may be a product of strong international pressure for "political correctness," and/or of the political calculation on the part of the successor States to be admitted smoothly into the international community.

What, then, is the result of this brief analysis? It could be summarized as follows: Human rights treaties do possess distinctive features: their legal regime can be said to differ in various regards from that of multilateral treaties whose obligations run (more) tangibly between the States parties.

On the other hand, these differences are not as profound as some observers among the human rights community appear to think. In particular, human rights treaties do not constitute "self-contained regimes" decoupled from the general law of treaties and of State responsibility.

CATHERINE REDGWELL*

Multilateral Environmental Treaty-Making

INTRODUCTION

Treaties are the most important source of international environmental law,[1] and constitute the primary method for creating rules and standards regulating the conduct of States and, indirectly, other actors in the environmental arena. Indeed, "the history of the development of environmental law ... can to a large extent be traced through the history of the conclusion of international agreements concerning environmental issues."[2] Writing in 1991, Weiss estimated that over 900 instruments,

* I would like to thank Professor Malgosia Fitzmaurice for her helpful comments on an earlier draft of this contribution.

1 For excellent discussion of the sources of international law from an environmental perspective, see further Patricia W. Birnie and Alan E. Boyle, *International Law & The Environment* (Oxford/New York, Clarendon Press/Oxford University Press, 1992), at pp. 9-29; see also Philippe Sands, Richard Tarasofsky and Mary Weiss, *Principles of International Environmental Law: Frameworks, Standards and Implementation* (Manchester/New York, Manchester University Press, 1995), ch. 4 ("International Law-making and Regulation"); Paul C. Szasz, "International Norm-making" in Edith Brown Weiss (ed.), *Environmental Change and International Law: New Challenges and Dimensions* (Transnational Publishers, 1992) at pp. 41-80; and M. A. Fitzmaurice, "International Environmental Law as a Special Field" (1994) XXV *Netherlands Yearbook of International Law,* pp. 181-226. For discussion of "Environmental Law: When Does It Make Sense to Negotiate International Agreements?" see *Proceedings of the 87th Annual Meeting of the American Society of International Law* (1993), Theme III "International Regimes: Progress and Problems", at pp. 377-397. See also the 1996 resolution of l'Institut de Droit international on environmental treaty making, Vol. 67-II, *Annuaire de l'Institut de Droit international*, session de Strasbourg, pp. 514-527.

2 Fitzmaurice, *ibid.*, at p. 187. One feature of this history of treaty-making reveals that, in common with the development of domestic environmental laws, treaty-making in the environmental field initially took a sectoral approach: see A.O. Adede, "Lessons from Twenty Years of International Law-Making in the Field of the Environment" in Alexandre Kiss and Françoise Burhenne-Guilmin (eds.), *A Law for the Environment: Essays in Honour of Wolfgang E. Burhenne* (IUCN/WCU, Gland/Cambridge, 1994), at p. 1; see also *ibid.*, "International Environmental Law from Stockholm to Rio – an Overview of Past Lessons and Future Challenges" (1992) 22/2 *Environmental Policy and Law,* pp. 88-105.

V. Gowlland-Debbas (ed.), Multilateral Treaty-making, 89–107.

multilateral and bilateral, had been concluded in the field[3]; the report to UNCED on the effectiveness of international environmental agreements examines 124 agreements and instruments, using UNEP's Register of International Treaties and Other Agreements in the Field of the Environment (1991)[4] as its point of departure.[5] Treaties can also be an important generator of customary international environmental law norms.[6]

The purpose of this contribution is to explore whether there is anything particularly distinctive about environmental treaty-making.[7] As the following will demonstrate, there are several key, but not necessarily unique, features of this process which can be identified, which are reflected in and even determinative of the form of treaty text adopted.

"PERMANENT" ENVIRONMENTAL DIPLOMACY

Treaty-making, particularly in the environmental field, is not necessarily a one-off event; rather, it is a process.[8] Negotiation leads not merely to the adoption of a

---

3 Edith Brown Weiss, "Environment and Trade as Partners in Sustainable Development: A Commentary" (1992) 86 AJIL, pp. 728-735. Palmer rightly points out that, while international environmental agreements may be impressive in number, the delay in ratification and entry into force, compliance, and the deteriorating state of the global environment, paint a less rosy picture. Geoffrey Palmer, "New Ways to Make International Environmental Law" (1992) 86 AJIL, pp. 259-283, at p. 263.

4 Since 1977, at the request of the United Nations General Assembly, the United Nations Environment Programme has maintained a "Register of International Treaties and Other Agreements in the Field of the Environment": see http://www.unep.org/ See also Bernd Rüster and Bruno Simma (eds.), *International Protection of the Environment: Treaties and Related Documents* (30 volumes 1975-1983, Dobbs Ferry NY, Oceana, with subsequent loose-leaf service). The CIESEN/SECAD/NASA maintained Environmental Treaties and Resources Indicators (ENTRI) lists over 170 instruments (which also includes non-binding instruments, such as OECD guidelines).

5 Peter H. Sand (ed.), *The Effectiveness of International Environmental Agreements: A Survey of Existing Legal Instruments* (Grotius, Cambridge, 1992). The agreements and instruments examined are listed in an Annex at pp. 501-538.

6 As Handl observes, customary international law has an important role to play here in the introduction of new concepts into international law which may challenge existing concepts, e.g. the challenge to national sovereignty posed by the concept of the common concern of humankind. See further Günther Handl, "Environmental Security and Global Change: the Challenge to International Law", (1990) 1 *Yearbook of International Environmental Law*, pp. 3-33.

7 Thus I will not consider here the broader issue of whether there is anything particularly distinctive about environmental treaties, an enquiry which necessarily would require consideration from negotiation through to termination.

8 A point which could equally be made about international law as a whole, viz. as process rather than (merely) rules: see further Rosalyn Higgins, *Problems and Process: International Law and How We Use It* (Clarendon Press, Oxford, 1994).

treaty text *simpliciter* but often constitutes an act of regime-creation.[9] In this sense the process of environmental treaty-making, the environmental "transaction", is relational rather than discrete.[10] As McConnell states at the end of her analysis of the negotiation of the 1992 Convention on Biological Diversity, once the text is negotiated the baton passes from negotiators to implementers in what she terms "the race to conserve the biodiversity of the planet's living resources".[11]

One of the characteristic features of international environmental law is thus the dynamic force of treaties which have been negotiated; that treaties are not one-off events but dynamic instruments which evolve over time. This is so particularly where institutional mechanisms for rule-making are established under the relevant treaty, such as the regular meetings of the Antarctic Treaty Consultative Parties under the 1959 Antarctic Treaty, but also where decisions of the Conference of the Parties have proven an effective and dynamic force in the evolution of the treaty, as for example has taken place under the 1989 Basle Convention on Transboundary Movement of Hazardous Waste.[12] It is this feature of environmental treaty-making which causes Gehring to point out that "institutionalizing stability" is not one of the objectives of such a process;[13] indeed, one might rather refer to the environ-

---

[9] Caldwell observes that "[t]he signing of a treaty customarily completes the first phase of a formalized effort toward institutionalized international environmental co-operation." Lynton K. Caldwell, "Beyond Environmental Diplomacy: the Changing Institutional Structure of International Co-operation" in John E. Carroll (ed.), *International Environmental Diplomacy: The Management and Resolution of Transfrontier Environmental Problems* (Cambridge University Press, Cambridge, 1988), ch. 1, at p. 20. See further Oran R. Young, *International Governance: Protecting the Environment in a Stateless Society* (Cornell University Press, Ithaca NY/London, 1994), at p. 27: "The provisions of international governance systems are ordinarily articulated explicitly in constitutional contracts that may, but need not, be codified in legally binding instruments such as conventions or treaties."

[10] To adopt the contract analysis of Professor Macneil in his critique of traditional contract doctrine's view of contract-making as a largely one-off event divorced from its social context. See Ian R. Macneil, "Relational Contract Theory as Sociology" (1987) 143 *Journal of Institutional and Theoretical Economics,* pp. 272-290.

[11] Fiona McConnell, *The Biodiversity Convention: A Negotiating History. A Personal Account of Negotiating the United Nations Convention on Biological Diversity – and After* (Kluwer Law International, London/The Hague, 1996), at p. 151. This analogy of baton-passing within a race is apt to the extent that negotiation, conclusion, implementation and enforcement of a treaty text may be perceived as existing on a continuum. Where the analogy is less apt is in terms of a finish line, for many environmental obligations cannot be defined (nor achieved) in absolute terms given their normative and frequently indeterminate nature.

[12] These are regimes with "semi-institutionalized multilateral rule-making frameworks". The legal regulation of hazardous waste also provides an example of inter-treaty regime building within what Kummer calls "the Basel Convention regime" including, *inter alia*, the 1972 London (Dumping) Convention and the soft law codes of the IAEA, as well as regional waste regulation: Katharina Kummer, *International Management of Hazardous Wastes: The Basel Convention and Related Legal Rules* (Clarendon Press, Oxford, 1995).

[13] Thomas Gehring, "International Environmental Regimes: Dynamic Sectoral Legal Systems" (1990) 1 *Yearbook of international Environmental Law,* pp. 35-56, at p.38.

mental treaty-making process as one of institutionalizing change. This perception of treaty-making as, *inter alia*, regime-creation[14] has led to considerable recent emphasis in international law and international relations literature upon global governance issues, constructing treaty negotiations as both norm- and institution/regime-creating exercises.[15]

A further distinction has been made between treaty-making directed towards regime-creation, and treaty-making within a regime.[16] The former takes place within a framework of general rules and principles whilst the latter develops within a framework of "internal law" and practice.[17] Whilst accepting this is a valid general distinction, it should be observed that particularly in times of conflict within regimes, protagonists will seek recourse to the set of rules supportive of the substantive outcome sought to be achieved, whether it is the general rules of the 1969 Vienna Convention on the Law of Treaties or the "internal law and practice" of treaty institutions.[18]

FLEXIBILITY IN FORM

One reason for the dynamic force of environmental treaties is the scientific basis for many of the substantive provisions of environmental treaty texts which will require amendment as new scientific knowledge comes to light. Political, social and economic developments may require similar flexibility. Flexibility in form is thus another hallmark of many international environmental treaties, most often reflected in framework treaties, with technical details relegated to protocols and/or annexes. General framework conventions will set out general obligations and provide for institutions (if any), but leave further concrete obligations to be established

---

[14] As to whether such regimes might be viewed as self-contained, see generally Bruno Simma, "Self-Contained Regimes" (1985) XVI *Netherlands Yearbook of International Law,* pp. 111-136; and (1994) XXV *Netherlands Yearbook of International Law passim*, in particular Fitzmaurice, *op. cit.*, n. 1.

[15] See for example Andrew Hurrell and Benedict Kingsbury (ed.), *The International Politics of the Environment: Actors, Interests and Institutions* (Clarendon Press/Oxford University Press, Oxford/New York, 1992) ("rules and regimes established to facilitate environmental co-operation").

[16] Winfried Lang, "Diplomacy and International Environmental Law-Making: Some Observations" (1992) 3 *Yearbook of International Environmental Law,* pp. 108-122, at p. 115; and pp. 117-122 (regime-building).

[17] *Ibid.*, at p. 115.

[18] A case in point is the 1946 International Convention for the Regulation of Whaling and the various treaty arguments employed by the pro- and anti- whaling lobbies in respect of the interpretation of the Convention: should general rules of treaty law apply or the "internal law and practice" of the parties, which has seen a rise in conservatory attitudes? With this and with other venerable living resources agreements, the issue arises of the extent to which an intertemporal approach may be taken to interpretation of its provisions. These are acute issues particularly given the rapid pace of change under many environmental agreements and the consequent apparent gulf between treaty language and treaty practice.

at some stage in the future. There are numerous environmental examples ranging from 1973/78 MARPOL[19] to the more recent 1992 Framework Convention on Climate Change with its 1997 Kyoto Protocol establishing targets and timetables for greenhouse gas reductions.[20] As Richardson observed in anticipation of the conclusion of the UNFCCC, "[t]o improve the chances of building a consensus around a framework treaty combining substantive and procedural elements, it should be stressed throughout the negotiations that its adoption will constitute only the first stage in a continuing process."[21]

In the maritime context this has been the approach followed by UNEP's Regional Seas programme.[22] Other examples include the global 1985 Vienna Convention for the Protection of the Ozone Layer, with the 1987 Montreal Protocol an excellent example of further elaboration,[23] and the regional 1979 UN/ECE Convention on Long-Range Transboundary Air Pollution (LRTAP) and its subsequent seven protocols on specific air pollutants with specific reduction targets and timetables.[24] This framework approach allows a step-by-step approach by States allowing "agreement" at the outset even where there is no consensus regarding the

---

[19] MARPOL 73/78 has six annexes covering different marine pollutants: Annexes I (oil) and II (noxious liquid substances in bulk) are mandatory for any State becoming party to MARPOL 73/78, with further annexes addressed to harmful substances carried in packages (Annex III); sewage (Annex IV); garbage (Annex V) and a sixth Annex, on air pollution from ships, adopted in 1997. The original 1973 Convention was revised in 1978 to facilitate entry into force, hence "MARPOL 73/78". Whilst MARPOL 73/78 provides the framework for its accompanying annexes, it is the 1982 LOSC which might be viewed as the general framework treaty on protection of the marine environment (Part XII) with MARPOL the specific substantive regulation of pollution from ships.

[20] See generally Peter G. G. Davies, "Global Warming and the Kyoto Protocol" (1998) 47 ICLQ, pp. 446-461 and http://www.unfccc.de/

[21] In Hurrell and Kingsbury (eds.), *op. cit.*, n. 15, at p. 172.

[22] Nine regional regimes have been established under UNEP's Regional Seas Programme, covering the Mediterranean, Black Sea, Wider Caribbean, Eastern African, Kuwait, Red Sea and Gulf of Aden, South Pacific, South-East Pacific, and West and Central African Regions. For further details see the *Yearbook of International Cooperation on Environment and Development 1998/99* (Fridtjof Nansen Institute, Earthscan, 1998) at pp. 118-137.

[23] See Winfried Lang, *op. cit.*, n.16, at p. 116. Further amendments to the 1987 Protocol have been made, most notably in 1990.

[24] The 1984 Protocol on Long-term Financing of the Co-operative Programme for Monitoring and Evaluation of the Long-range Transmission of Air Pollutants in Europe (EMEP); the 1985 Protocol on the Reduction of Sulphur Emissions or their Transboundary Fluxes by at least 30 per cent; the 1988 Protocol concerning the Control of Emissions of Nitrogen Oxides or their Transboundary Fluxes; the 1991 Protocol on the Control of Emissions of Volatile Organic Compounds or their Transboundary Fluxes; the 1994 Protocol on Further Reduction of Sulphur Emissions; the 1998 Protocol on Heavy Metals; and the 1998 Protocol on Persistent Organic Pollutants. For texts see http://www.unece.org/env/lrtap. A further protocol, known as the "multi-effect, multi-pollutant agreement" is under negotiation (1999) which sets new national emission limits on key air pollutants (SO2, NH3, NOx and VOCs) to reduce acidification, eutrophication and ozone pollution.

concrete steps to be taken to address a particular environmental problem.[25] This can create its own momentum, leading to the conclusion of further Protocols as the Barcelona Regional Seas Convention for the Mediterranean,[26] and the 1979 LRTAP Convention and its Protocols, attest. Levy rightly identifies this two-stage process as one of consensus-building and rule-making,[27] though these processes are not necessarily sequential with consensus-building a continuing process buttressing, *inter alia*, the conclusion of subsequent protocols. It has been suggested that there is some danger that the first step, viz. of concluding a framework agreement, may lead to stagnation as the impetus for further measures is lost – the "this problem has been dealt with" phenomenon, or the appearance of doing something when in fact no concrete obligations have been undertaken,[28] though the evidence suggests that this attitude, whilst delaying subsequent rule-making, does not necessarily prevent it altogether. Rather, a new dilemma looms and that is the phenomenon of treaty congestion or proliferation, giving rise to the real possibility of intra-treaty as well as of inter-treaty conflicts. This has led to criticism of what is perceived as perpetual re-inventing of the wheel, and a call for some form of international co-ordination or overview by UNEP or a revamped Trusteeship Council.[29]

---

25 LRTAP is a particularly good example of this, with only two of the participating States (Norway and Sweden) initially convinced of the need for stringent reductions in SO2 to prevent acid rain: see further E. Fouéré, "Emerging trends in international environmental agreements" in John E. Carroll, ed., *op. cit.,* n.9, ch. 3, at pp. 35-36; and Marc A. Levy, "European Acid Rain: The Power of Tote-Board Diplomacy", in Peter M. Haas, Robert O. Keohane and Marc A. Levy (eds.), *Institutions for the Earth: Sources of Effective International Environmental Protection* (The MIT Press, Cambridge MA/London, 1993), ch. 3, at p. 76.

26 The Barcelona Convention was amended in 1995: see the Convention for the Protection of the Marine Environment and Coastal Region of the Mediterranean, adopted 10 June 1995, amending the 1976 Convention. Six Protocols have been added to the Convention, addressed to hazardous waste (1996), pollution from continental shelf exploration and exploitation (1994), specially protected areas (1982), land-based pollution (1980), oil and other harmful substances in emergencies (1976) and dumping (1976). The Barcelona Convention has been viewed as a prototype for the other regional seas agreements concluded under UNEP's regional seas programme, listed at n.22 above. See, generally, Peter H. Sand, *Marine Environment Law in the United Nations Environment Programme: An Emergent Eco-Regime* (Tycooly Publ., London/New York, 1988).

27 *Op. cit.*, n.25, at p. 76; with LRTAP "out of weakness came strength". He notes that perhaps only two of the original 30 Contracting Parties to LRTAP considered acid rain an environmental problem, thus underscoring the consensus-building attributes of the treaty.

28 Susskind and Ozawa suggest a further problem – that the lowest common denominator will prevail (or the laggard state problem) – not a problem unique to environmental treaties, of course. Lawrence Susskind and Connie Ozawa, in Hurrell and Kingsbury (eds.), *op. cit.*, n.15, at p. 147; see also Lawrence E. Susskind, *Environmental Diplomacy: Negotiating More Effective Environmental Agreements* (Oxford University Press, Oxford/New York, 1994).

29 See further Geoffrey Palmer, *op. cit.* n.3; for discussion of institutional proposals see further this author, *Intergenerational Trusts and Environmental Protection* (Juris/MUP, 1999).

Amendment procedures in environmental treaties[30] frequently distinguish between amendment of substantive provisions of the treaty, which generally require unanimity or a significant majority (typically two-thirds or three-quarters of the Contracting Parties), and amendment of technical regulations, set out in a separate schedule, annex or appendix or protocol, where a lower threshold of a simple or qualified majority for amendment will be required. Thus necessary flexibility may be embodied in the adoption of technical annexes which may be more readily amended. This technique is common in living resource conventions, e.g. the 1946 International Convention for the Regulation of Whaling; in respect of waste disposal at sea (1972 Oslo and 1972 London (Dumping) Conventions);[31] and in hazardous waste treaties such as the 1989 Basel Convention on the Transboundary Movement of Hazardous Waste. Indeed, three tiers may emerge: a framework treaty, additional protocol(s) with annexes embodying technical details which may be easily updated and amended.[32] The technique of a lower threshold for adoption is frequently coupled with a negative opt-out procedure which places the onus on an objecting party to so object (so-called tacit acceptance). Thus, for example, Article 30 of the 1992 Biodiversity Convention permits an annex, once adopted by

---

30 See, generally, M.J. Bowman, "The Multilateral Treaty Amendment Process – A Case Study" (1995) 44 ICLQ, pp. 540-559 (with case study of the Ramsar Convention on Wetlands of International Importance).

31 The dumping of waste at sea is one example of a framework convention following specific sectoral/regional regulation. The 1972 London (Dumping) Convention and further regional agreements are to be read in the light of the essentially framework provisions of the 1982 LOSC. There is cross-referencing in the LDC to the (then) forthcoming law of the sea negotiations, whilst Part XII of the LOSC is clearly drafted with reference to existing detailed international and regional treaties on various aspects of marine pollution.

32 As Bowman observes, "Such structures may generate a need for an equally sophisticated array of amendment procedures, differentially tailored according to the levels of obligation." *Op. cit.*, n.30, at p. 542. A variation on this tiered structure is treaty, annex, appendix and decision. See, for example, the 1992 Convention on the Protection of the Marine Environment of the North-East Atlantic ("OSPAR"), which is a framework treaty with five detailed Annexes and a number of appendices, the latter expressly stated to be of a scientific, technical or administrative nature (Article 14). Separate provisions are included for the amendment of the Convention (Article 15), and for the adoption and amendment of Annexes (Articles 16 and 17) and of Appendices (Articles 18 and 19). The treaty provides for the binding force of decisions where certain procedural requirements are met, namely, after the expiry of 200 days for those parties which voted for the decision and which have not indicated within this period that the decision is no longer accepted (Article 13). De La Fayette observes that the decision route may be used for "indirect amendments of the Convention by a faster and more flexible route than the formal amendment procedure in Article 15." Louise de La Fayette, "The OSPAR Convention Comes into Force: Continuity and Progress" (1999) 14 *International Journal of Marine and Coastal Law,* pp. 247-297, at p. 257. The move to prohibit the dumping, and the leaving wholly or partly in place, of disused offshore installations, embodied in Decision 98/3 (in force 9 February 1999), might be viewed in this light.

the Contracting Parties, to enter into force one year after adoption unless a Contracting Party otherwise notifies the Depositary, in writing, within this period.[33]

The Antarctic Treaty is an interesting example of several methods combined: a substantive treaty text concluded in 1959, dynamically evolved through regular meetings of the parties (with the special role of the Antarctic Treaty Consultative Parties), subsequent related agreements[34] and a 1991 Environmental Protocol to the Antarctic Treaty which embodies technical details in annexes thereto (which in fact elevate many of the previous decisions of the ATCPs to treaty status).[35] This is the ultimate in flexibility: a framework agreement (though it must be said that the Antarctic Treaty embodies significant rules), a Protocol and further annexes embodying technical details, supplemented by rule-making by the ATCPs.[36] Together these comprise the Antarctic Treaty System – regime building par excellence, creating inter-linked treaty institutions held together within the system through the common thread of participation by the ATCPs.

THE SCIENTIFIC BASIS FOR ENVIRONMENTAL TREATIES

At the outset, the complexities and often uncertainties of science can raise problems of scope in international negotiations.[37] What should be included? Excluded?

---

33 See also *ibid.* (OSPAR Convention).

34 In addition to the 1959 Antarctic Treaty and the 1991 Environmental Protocol, the Antarctic Treaty System comprises the 1978 Convention on the Conservation of Seals and the 1982 Convention on the Conservation of Antarctic Marine Living Resources. The 1988 Convention on the Regulation of Antarctic Mineral Resource Activities is now defunct in consequence of the 50-year moratorium on Antarctic mineral resource activities embodied in the 1991 Protocol.

35 For further discussion of the Protocol and its annexes, see this author, "Environmental Protection in Antarctica: the 1991 Protocol" (1994) 43 ICLQ, pp. 599-634.

36 Decision 1 (1995) established that legally binding provisions adopted by the ATCPs will be expressed as "measures" whilst "decisions" will regulate internal organizational matters; the format of "resolution" is reserved for purely hortatory texts.

37 The complexity of environmental negotiations may also lead to a considerable lead-in time from initiation through negotiation to the adoption of the treaty text, with a further period elapsing before the entry into force of the treaty. A good example is the 1982 Law of the Sea Convention, negotiated from 1973-1982 and which entered into force in 1994. In marked contrast is both the 1992 Biodiversity and Climate Change Conventions, which took less than two years to negotiate and which entered into force very rapidly (1993 and 1994 respectively). There are, of course, many key points of distinction between these texts, not least the tremendous breadth and complexity of the LOSC which is a rule-making and codification treaty par excellence, whilst both the Climate Change and Biodiversity Conventions are more framework in character. Other key points of distinction are levels of political support and the entry into force requirements of the treaties. In respect of the former, both the Biodiversity and Climate Change Conventions enjoyed high levels of political support particularly given the coincidence of the 1992 Rio Conference on Environment and Development with the period for signature. Entry into force of the Law of the Sea Convention, on the other hand, was delayed by concerns by some industrialized States regarding the operation of Part XI (addressed via the treaty mechanism of the 1994 Agreement on Imple-

Global warming provides a particularly good example of an environmental problem caused by a wide range of human activities that also vary from country to country in terms of relative contribution to the problem. How to decide what to include in, and what to leave outside of, the Convention? The availability of reliable scientific data, and the capacity to monitor, are scientific or technical factors which will influence negotiations, alongside a wide range of economic, social and political factors. Essentially, however, there needs to be "a widely shared scientific consensus on the nature of the problem and its solutions".[38] The role of the IPPC in shaping perceptions of greenhouse gases causing global warming has been a key one in this regard.

Scientific uncertainty will not necessarily prevent agreement; rather it puts emphasis upon the need for information gathering and exchange, monitoring and reporting obligations, in the treaty text. This again influences what form the agreement will take, with a push towards the framework treaty embodying these essentially procedural requirements,[39] with subsequent protocols embodying more substantive commitments based on data generated through the first generation of monitoring and reporting obligations. The Climate Change Convention and Kyoto Protocol, and the LRTAP Convention and its protocols, are good examples of this phenomenon. Scientific uncertainty – chronic in the environmental as other fields [40] – has also been generative of new principles such as prevention and, more recently, the precautionary principle.[41]

The irreversibility of many types of environmental harm (e.g. global warming, species extinction) likewise places emphasis upon prevention, precaution, and effective standards-setting, implementation and enforcement and procedural obligations to notify, consult and warn of harm. It also illuminates the limited usefulness of liability and compensation regimes where harm is irreversible. Liability and responsibility are underdeveloped areas in international environmental law with relatively few examples of specific liability regimes.[42] Examples include nuclear

---

mentation). Moreover, the LOSC required 60 ratifications to enter into force, whilst the Biodiversity Convention required 30 ratifications and the Climate Change 50 ratifications.

38 A. Hurrell and B. Kingsbury, "The International Politics of the Environment: An Introduction" in *ibid.*, *op. cit.*, n. 15, at p. 19.

39 See, generally, Phoebe Okowa, "Procedural Obligations in International Environmental Agreements" (1996) 67 BYIL, pp. 275-336. The first protocol to LRTAP, EMEP, provided an essential foundation for the development of further protocols embodying specific targets and timetables in respect of particular air pollutants.

40 This flows as much from the nature of scientific knowledge as from specific environmental phenomena. On the former see Thomas S. Kuhn, *The Structure of Scientific Revolutions* (2nd enlarged edition, University of Chicago Press Chicago/London, reprint of Foundations of the Unity of Science series, Vol. II No. 2, 1970).

41 See further David Freestone and Ellen Hey (eds.) *The Precautionary Principle and International Law: The Challenge of Implementation* (Kluwer Law International, The Hague/London, 1996).

42 For discussion of the development of liability regimes in the regional marine pollution context, see R. Lefeber, "Liability in Regional Marine Conventions: Dead Letters in

activities,[43] oil pollution,[44] hazardous and noxious substances,[45] and hazardous waste.[46]

TRANSBOUNDARY CHARACTER OF ENVIRONMENTAL ISSUES

The oft-cited reasons for multilateral action in the environmental sphere scarcely need be rehearsed – the transboundary character of many environmental problems, and/or degradation of the global commons requiring concerted international environmental action for amelioration. Whilst the transboundary character of environmental problems is well-appreciated, and the need to protect areas beyond national jurisdiction, a significant recent development is the appreciation of environmental problems of global proportions requiring action within national borders for the benefit of the international community as a whole.[47] Problems of such magnitude are generally identified and addressed in international treaties which require for effectiveness widespread state participation to ensure that the problem is addressed and that the benefits accrue to the international community as a whole. Protection of the ozone layer, climate change and conservation of biological diversity are recent examples of this phenomenon.[48]

A further need for multilateral action in standards-setting arises not only because unilateral action is ineffective to address transboundary and global environmental problems, but also because such action may lead to competitive distortions.

---

the Sea", in Davor Vidas and Willy Østreng (eds.), *Order for the Oceans at the Turn of the Century* (Kluwer Law International, The Hague/Boston 1999).

43 See, for example, the regional 1960 Paris Convention on Third Party Liability in the Field of Nuclear Energy, with its 1963 Brussels Supplementary Convention, and the global Vienna Convention on Civil Liability for Nuclear Damage, linked by a 1988 Joint Protocol.

44 See, for example, the 1969 International Convention on Civil Liability for Oil Pollution Damage and the 1971 Convention on the Establishment of an International Fund for Compensation for Oil Pollution Damage, both updated in 1992 by Protocols.

45 See the 1996 International Convention on Liability and Compensation for Damage in Connection with the Carriage of Hazardous and Noxious Substances by Sea.

46 Parties to the 1989 Basel Convention on the Transboundary Movement of Hazardous Wastes and their Disposal are negotiating a Protocol on Liability and Compensation for Damage, a draft text of which will be forwarded to the fifth meeting of the Conference of the Parties in December 1999.

47 Rüdiger Wolfrum, "Purposes and Principles of International Environmental Law" (1990) 33 GYIL, pp. 308-330, at p. 327; see also Jutta Brunnée, "'Common Interest' – Echoes from an Empty Shell? Some Thoughts on Common Interests and International Environmental Law" (1989) 49 ZaöRV, pp. 791-808, at p. 794 *et seq*. As Wolfrum observes, the process of identification of environmental problems of global significance raises a number of issues, including the competence of the identifier: *ibid.*, at p. 328.

48 Writing in 1990, Wolfrum cites the examples of the 1972 World Heritage Convention, the Ozone Convention, Ramsar and CITES in this connection: *ibid.*, at pp. 327-328.

Concerted action reduces or even eliminates the free rider phenomenon; however, the benefits of such action may be diffuse and burdens not equally shared if not all, or at least most, States participate. This leads to pressure to internationalize standards and to achieve widespread participation. This is especially evident in the pollution context, where level playing field arguments can predominate (I'll do it if all of my competitors do it); however, this argument has a further equitable dimension in that requiring adherence to common standards without differentiation has the effect, *inter alia*, of perpetuating existing distortions and may be perceived as inequitable. This has given rise to a new approach of "common but differentiated responsibilities", and of international concern to address a non-legal factor, namely, the economic costs of environmental regulation, which may affect compliance with and the effectiveness of international environmental agreements.

Differentiating Obligations and Differentiating Responsibilities

There are many ways in which obligations may be differentiated under a treaty. Several are multilateral in character, e.g. it is agreed by the parties that certain of them will adhere to different standards, or apply the same standards but with a grace period for implementation (temporal and/or substantive derogations), or that opt-outs will be permitted.[49] This process has been referred to as "softening obligations".[50] Thus it is not the case that in the presence of a prohibition on reservations an environmental treaty will necessarily impose uniform obligations on all contracting parties irrespective of circumstance. The standard method for unilateral differentiation, viz. where individual Contracting Parties choose the extent of their obligations under a treaty to the extent permitted by it, is through reservations.[51] However, partly in consequence of the nature of environmental negotiations, which are as much a process of consensus building as seeking agreement on a written text, and in consequence of the increasing use of consensus as the basis for adopting a treaty text, modern multilateral environmental treaties do not generally permit reservations. The path-breaking example in this regard is undoubtedly the Third United Nations Conference on the Law of the Sea, the first major treaty conference to utilize the consensus technique as its modus operandi and to adopt a package-

---

[49] See, for example, the grace period for developing countries contained in Article 5 of the Montreal Protocol. Article 175 EC also allows for temporary derogation from measures which impose a disproportionate cost on the public authorities of a Member State. Further latitude may be afforded Member States in individual directives, for example the derogations afforded to Spain under the large combustion plant directive. See further Joanne Scott, *EC Environmental Law* (Longmans, London, 1998), pp. 37-43, esp. p. 39 ("shared but differentiated responsibilities").

[50] Lang, *op. cit.*, n.16, at p. 116.

[51] See further D. W. Bowett, "Reservations to Non-Restricted Multilateral Treaties" (1976-7) 48 BYIL, pp. 67-92; this author, (1993) 65 BYIL, pp. 245-282.

deal approach to the text as a whole. [52] The latter approach had an "integrative effect on the negotiations". [53] Unsurprisingly therefore, Article 309 LOSC prohibits general reservations. Similar prohibition is found in many recent environmental treaties such as the 1985 Convention for the Protection of the Ozone Layer (Article 18) and 1990 Montreal Protocol (Article 18); the 1989 Basel Convention on the Control of Transboundary Movement of Hazardous Wastes and their Disposal (Article 26); the 1992 Climate Change Convention (Article 24) and 1997 Kyoto Protocol (Article 26); the 1992 Biodiversity Convention (Article 37); the 1992 Convention for the Protection of the Marine Environment of the North-East Atlantic (Article 28); the 1995 Agreement for the Implementation of the Provisions of the United Nations Convention on the Law of the Sea of 10 December 1982 Relating to the Conservation and Management of Straddling Fish Stocks and Highly Migratory Fish Stocks (Article 42). Unlike the 1982 LOSC, not all of these Conventions have adopted a "package deal" approach. However, the need to preserve consensus surrounding even only a framework agreement or the substantive commitments of, say, an associated protocol (Montreal and Kyoto for example), will encourage protection from blanket reservations.

But there is a further reason, and that is the recent development in the environmental sphere of the concept of "common but differentiated responsibilities".[54] This replaces individual differentiation via the reservations route with a form of multilateralised differentiation, agreed by all contracting parties in negotiations but applicable only to those contracting parties meeting the criteria for differentiation.[55] This reflects the need to take into account the different capacities of States in global regime building and different contributions historically to existing environmental pollution problems in particular. "Common but differentiated responsibility" is also a reflection of the desirability for universalizing obligations. For example, while the Climate Convention prohibits reservations (Article 24), it differentiates in respect of burden-sharing in achieving the common purpose of the Convention. Article 3(1) accordingly provides that "developed country Parties should take the lead in combating climate change and the adverse effects thereof". This is further amplified in the concrete obligations undertaken by developed

---

[52] On the procedural innovations of UNCLOS III see Albert W. Koers, "The Third United Nations Conference on the Law of the Sea – some remarks on its contribution towards the making of international law", in Wybo P. Heere (ed.), *International Law and its Source: Liber Amicorum Maarten Bos* (Kluwer Law and Taxation Publ., Deventer/Antwerp, 1989), at pp. 23-46.

[53] *Ibid.*, at p. 34.

[54] See Principle 7 of the Rio Declaration and Article 3(1) of the Climate Change Convention; for further discussion see, generally, Daniel B. Magraw, "Legal Treatment of Developing Countries: Differential, Contextual and Absolute Norms" (1990) 1 *Colorado Journal of International Environmental Law & Policy,* pp. 69-99; and R. Mushkat, "Environmental Sustainability: A Perspective from the Asia-Pacific Region" (1993) 27 UBC Law Review, p. 153, at p. 161.

[55] Further evidence of multilateralism is evident in the new approach to dispute settlement through non-compliance procedures, discussed further below (point 9).

country Parties under the Kyoto Protocol.[56] The purpose of such differentiation is to reflect existing inequities within the international system, and to encourage developing country participation but without undermining the common purpose of the Convention. This finds distinct echoes in the classic argument in favour of unilateral differentiation through the reservations route, viz., that allowing reservations facilitates wider participation in the treaty text. This goes right back to the Genocide Convention Case in 1951, where the ICJ adopted an object and purpose test in respect of reservations to encourage widespread participation, but not at the expense of the core integrity of the treaty. Wider participation is crucial to the effectiveness of international environmental agreements. Over two-thirds of environmental treaties have been concluded since the Stockholm Conference in 1972, yet there is still a marked "clustering" of membership by developed States; this imbalance is also reflected in the governance structures of existing agreements and instruments.[57]

FACILITATIVE FINANCING AND TECHNOLOGY TRANSFER

One mechanism for improving participation is the evolution of facilitative financing through financial mechanisms such as trust fund arrangements.[58] Examples may be found under the 1979 Migratory Species Convention; the Ramsar Convention on Conservation of Wetlands, the Barcelona Convention, and the World Heritage Convention. More recently, the financial mechanisms of the Montreal Protocol to the 1985 Ozone Layer Convention and of the 1992 Biodiversity and Climate Change Conventions have seen the establishment of a Global Environmental Facility to assist developing States with the cost of implementing and complying with their treaty obligations.[59] This reflects the origins of such mechanisms as burden sharing in respect of the agreed incremental costs of implementation,[60]

---

56 For further discussion, see Davies, *op. cit.*, n.20.

57 Sand, Summary Report of Survey, *op. cit.*, n.5, at p. 11. He observes further, based on the 124 agreements and instruments surveyed, that technical and financial assistance are crucial elements in facilitating developing State participation. This is considered further below.

58 For comprehensive analysis of conservation trust funds for biodiversity conservation supported by the Global Environmental Facility, see GEF, *Evaluation of Experience with Conservation Trust Funds* (November, 1998).

59 The GEF provides incremental funding for projects in four key areas: biodiversity, climate change, international waters, and ozone depletion. It is the designated financial mechanism under the Biodiversity and Climate Change Conventions; the Montreal Protocol has its own Multilateral Fund to assist developing countries with the costs of phasing out production and consumption of ozone-depleting substances, but the GEF is able to assist States which do not meet the Fund's criteria, (mainly economies in transition). For further details see http://www.gefweb.com.

60 The financial mechanisms of the CBD and FCCC are excellent examples both of facilitative financing and also improved governance structures. The GEF Governing Council does not operate along the lines of the World Bank or IMF but rather has equitable repre-

with a broader focus than merely financial provision.[61] Such mechanisms are express acknowledgement of the cost, and of the economic feasibility, of environmental regulatory measures.[62] Adede refers to the inclusion of such mechanisms as one of the characteristics of the "new breed of environmental treaties" which, *inter alia*, address more directly the rights and interests of developing States.[63]

A further key facilitator is the transfer of technology and of expertise.[64] The former in particular has proved controversial, most notably perhaps in the transfer of technology provisions of the 1982 LOSC (Article 144) which were subsequently modified by the 1994 Implementation Agreement (Annex, Section 5) due to opposition from a number of developed States. This was also a controversial subject in negotiating the Biodiversity Convention, Article 16 of which is addressed to access to and transfer of technology (including biotechnology), in part owing to concerns regarding intellectual property rights.[65] Provisions on technology transfer are also found in the Climate Change Convention (Article 4), with the Kyoto Protocol reaffirming the commitment of developed state parties to funding such technology transfer.

GLOBAL ACTORS, COMMUNITY INTERESTS

Undoubtedly international environmental law has seen a proliferation in the number and range of actors in the environmental sphere, in particular non-

sentation with 16 representatives from developing countries, 14 from developed countries, and 2 from economies in transition. For background to the restructuring of the GEF, see S. Johnstone, "Financial Aid, Biodiversity and International Law", in Michael Bowman and Catherine Redgwell (eds.), *International Law and the Conservation of Biological Diversity* (Kluwer Law International, London/The Hague, 1996).

61 The GEF Report, *op. cit.* n.58, at p. 10, emphasizes that conservation trust funds are more than financial mechanisms, but "institutions" with a key role to play in developing national conservation strategies, in providing technical expertise, and in capacity building within local NGO communities. Indeed, NGOs, the private sector, and the scientific community are important players in the design and implementation of GEF-financed projects in all four areas of activity.

62 See also Lang, *op. cit.*, n.16, at p. 122.

63 Adede, *op. cit.*, n.2, at p. 13.

64 See, for example, Article 12 of the Biodiversity Convention which provides for research and training "taking into account the special needs of developing countries"; see also, more generally, Principle 9 of the 1992 Rio Declaration (exchange of scientific and technical knowledge, transfer of technologies).

65 Article 16(5) merely notes that patents and other intellectual property rights may have an impact on the implementation of the Convention and exhorts Contracting Parties to co-operate to ensure that such rights support, rather than run counter, to the objectives of the Convention. For an overview of the issues, see I. Walden, "Intellectual Property Rights and Biodiversity", in Bowman and Redgwell (eds.), *op. cit.*, n.60. On the Convention generally, see further (1997) 6:3 RECIEL *passim*.

governmental actors (NGOs).[66] Witness the number of actors identified in Agenda 21: section 3 on "strengthening the role of major groups" addresses women; children and youth; indigenous peoples[67]; NGOs; local authorities; workers and their trade unions; business and industry; the scientific and technological community; and farmers.[68] The role of NGOs in particular has been significant both in shaping the treaty negotiating process but also in stimulating subsequent developments within treaty regimes. This is achieved primarily through the mechanism of participation, viz. as observers in international organizations and in treaty negotiations. This is part of a wider trend towards viewing international society in terms broader than a community of States alone.[69] It is recognized in recent environmental treaties such as the Climate Change and Biodiversity Conventions, where these environmental issues are recognized as the common concern of humankind.[70] The role of international organizations such as UNEP, IMO, FAO and the ECE in the environmental law-making process is also considerable, particularly in facilitating intergovernmental treaty-making.[71]

The participation of non-State actors has also been encouraged by a general shift from command-and-control regulation to the use of economic instruments and other devices, e.g. taxes, tradeable permits, labelling, auditing and management schemes.[72] This has led to increased use of self-regulation, industry and consumer-

---

66 See L.K. Caldwell, "Beyond Environmental Diplomacy: the Changing Institutional Structure of International Co-operation", in John E. Carroll (ed.), *op. cit.*, n.9, at pp. 19-20 and 22-24 (environmental NGOs' participation from initiation to negotiation through to ratification and implementation); Philippe Sands, *op. cit.*, n.1, ch. 3; and *ibid.*, "The Environment, Community and International Law" (1989) 30 *Harvard International Law Journal,* pp. 393-420.

67 The important role of indigenous peoples is explicitly recognized in the Biodiversity Convention: see Article 8(j). COP4 established an ad hoc open-ended inter-sessional working group on the implementation of this provision.

68 Nicholas A. Robinson (ed.), *Agenda 21: Earth's Action Plan* (Oceana, New York/London, 1993), chs. 23-32; see also Principles 20-22 of the 1992 Rio Declaration.

69 See, for example, Commission on Global Governance, *Our Global Neighbourhood* (Oxford/New York, Oxford University Press, 1995); and, on the intersection between human rights and the environment, Alan E. Boyle and Michael R. Anderson (eds.), *Human Rights Approaches to Environmental Protection* (Clarendon Press, Oxford, 1996).

70 On the legal significance of "common concern of humankind", see Alan E. Boyle, "International Law and the Protection of the Global Atmosphere: Concepts, Categories and Principles", in Robin Churchill and David Freestone (eds.), *International Law and Climate Change* (Graham & Trotman/Martinus Nijhoff, London/Dordrecht, 1991), at pp. 7-19. On whether international environmental law is anthropocentric in approach, see this author, "Life, the Universe and Everything: A Critique of Anthropocentric Rights", in Boyle and Anderson, *ibid.*, ch. 4, at pp. 71-87.

71 For example, the promotion and progressive development of international environmental law is one of UNEP's major functions. See further Julia Sommer, "Environmental Law-Making by International Organizations" (1996) 56/3 ZaöRV pp. 628-667.

72 See, generally, Anthony Ogus, *Regulation: Legal Form and Economic Theory* (Clarendon Press/Oxford University Press, Oxford/New York, 1994); this author, "Privatization and Environmental Regulation: Some Observations", in Klaus Bosselmann and Ben-

based, and other voluntary systems for compliance. These essentially domestic regulatory trends have been mirrored at the EC and international levels, stimulated in part by the desire for transnational harmonization of such standards.[73] The further development of the flexibility mechanisms under the Kyoto Protocol – joint implementation, clean development mechanism, and most importantly, tradeable emission permits – will continue this trend towards the increased participation of non-State actors.[74]

ROLE OF SOFT LAW[75]/NON-TREATIES[76]

It is due to the nature of environmental problems and their regulation that traditional methods of diplomacy, with lengthy and costly treaty-making procedures,

---

jamin J. Richardson (ed.), *Environmental Justice and Market Mechanisms: Key Challenges for Environmental Law and Policy* (Kluwer Law International, The Hague/London, 1999); and Alfred Rest, "New Legal Instruments for Environmental Prevention, Control and Restoration in Public International Law" (1993) 23 *Environmental Policy and Law,* pp. 260-272 (with discussion of enhanced co-operation between State and industry).

[73] See further Naomi Roht-Arriaza, "Private Voluntary Standard-Setting, the International Organization for Standardization, and International Environmental Law Making" (1995) 6 *Yearbook of International Environmental Law,* pp. 107-163; and *ibid.* "Shifting the Point of Regulation: The International Organization for Standardization and Global Lawmaking in Trade and Environment" (1995) 22 *Ecology Law Quarterly,* p. 479, at pp. 532-534 (influence of private standards-setting on public international law-making, with particular reference to oil pollution and to pesticides control).

[74] See (1998) 7:2 RECIEL *passim*; L. Campbell, "Emission Trading, Joint Implementation and the Clean Development Mechanism: The Role of Private Sector and Other Non-State Actors in Implementation", in W. Bradnee Chambers (ed.), *Global Climate Governance: Inter-linkages between the Kyoto Protocol and other Multilateral Regimes* (UNU/IAS/GEIC, 1998); see also Worika, Brown, Vinogradov and Waelde, "Contractual Aspects of Implementing the Clean Development Mechanisms under the Kyoto Protocol", and Werksman and Santoro, "Investing in Sustainable Development: the Potential Interaction Between the Kyoto Protocol and a Multilateral Agreement on Investment", *ibid.*

[75] See further Alan Boyle's contribution, *infra.*; see also Pierre-Marie Dupuy, "Soft Law and the International Law of the Environment" (1991) 12 *Michigan Journal of International Law,* pp. 420-435; P. Birnie, in H. Ringbom (eds.), *Competing Norms in the Law of Marine Environmental Protection: Focus on Ship Safety and Pollution Prevention* (Kluwer Law International, London/Boston, 1997); and, generally, C.M. Chinkin, "The Challenge of Soft Law. Development and Change in International law" (1989) 38 ICLQ, pp. 850-866.

[76] An excellent example of a "non-treaty" is the memorandum of understanding: see, generally, Anthony Aust "The Theory and Practice of Informal International Instruments", (1986) 35 ICLQ, pp. 787-812. Environmental examples include MOUs for inter-institutional cooperation, e.g. MOU between CITES Secretariat and INTERPOL, and for harmonizing the exercise of port state enforcement of existing international standards (e.g. under MARPOL 73/78). For further discussion see F. Plaza, "Port State control: an update"(1997) 4 IMO News, p. 30; for a chart of existing MOUs, commencing with the 1982 Paris Memorandum of Understanding on Port State Control, see *ibid.*, at p. 34.

have been augmented in the environmental field by more speedy and flexible mechanisms for treaty-creation and change. Not only are transaction costs reduced but, as Kiss observes, soft law provides a platform for consensus-building and for subsequent regime building by facilitating a step-by-step approach.[77] The particular role which soft law may play in paving the way for the subsequent conclusion of a binding treaty text is seen in the example of UNEP's Cairo Guidelines and Principles for the Environmentally Sound Management of Hazardous Waste (1987) reflected in the 1989 Basel Convention on the Control of Transboundary Movements of Hazardous Wastes. In similar fashion, soft law may facilitate further growth within a regime, such as the Sofia Declaration which preceded conclusion of the NOx Protocol to LRTAP or the 1989 Helsinki Declaration laying the groundwork for the 1990 amendments to the 1987 Montreal Protocol to the Ozone Layer Convention.[78] Frequently identified also is the possibility for soft law instruments to embody more detailed provisions than might otherwise be agreed in binding format[79] though the frailties of such an approach are obvious. Soft law is also a particularly useful technique for bodies which are not recognized as law-creating entities as such, e.g. NGOs, and/or where States may be in a minority or, as is the case in establishing business codes of conduct, entirely absent.[80]

NON-COMPLIANCE PROCEDURES [81]

As part of the trend towards multilateralism already noted above, there is an increasing tendency to rely on alternative methods for dispute resolution and for achieving compliance. This reflects a community interest in securing observance of treaty norms which are for the ultimate benefit of that community, and reflects the

---

77 Alexandre Kiss, "Nouvelles tendances en droit de l'environnement" (1989) 32 GYBIL, pp. 241-263. See also Adede, *op. cit.*, n.2, at p. 14, who identifies six categories of use of soft law instruments in environmental law-making over the past twenty years.

78 On the latter see Palmer, *op. cit.*, n.3, at pp. 269-70.

79 Adede, *op. cit.*, n.2, at p.15; see also the ASIL Proceedings, *op. cit.*. n.1.

80 *Ibid.*, at p. 11; Roht-Arriaza, *op. cit.*, n.73, at pp. 138-146; and, generally, Peter H. Sand, *Lessons Learned in Global Environmental Governance* (World Resources Institute, Washington D.C., 1990). As Roht-Arriaza points out, however, the "non-state dominated nature of the standard-setting process does not necessarily guarantee adequate representation for societal interests" raising concerns, *inter alia*, regarding the legitimacy of the process. *Ibid.*, at p. 140.

81 See, generally, Martti Koskenniemi, "Breach of a Treaty or Non-Compliance? Reflections on Enforcement of the Montreal Protocol" (1992) 3 *Yearbook of International Environmental Law,* pp. 123-162; Patrick Széll, "The Development of Multilateral Mechanisms for Monitoring Compliance" in Winfried Lang (eds.), *Sustainable Development and International Law* (Graham & Trotman/Martinus Nijhoff, London/Dordrecht, 1995) at pp. 97-109; James Cameron, Jacob Werksman and Peter Roderick (eds.), *Improving Compliance with International Environmental Law* (Earthscan, London, 1996); and this author, "Non-Compliance Procedures and the Climate Change Convention", in Chambers (ed.), *op. cit.* n.74.

generally non-reciprocal character of multilateral environmental treaty obligations. It is also a reflection of the growing awareness that traditional rules of international law concerned with material breach of treaty obligations and with state responsibility are inappropriate to address problems of environmental treaty implementation. Gehring views the growth of such non-compliance procedures as an internalization of the judicial function;[82] indeed, the use of internal treaty mechanisms to address non-compliance may also be seen as part of the increasing role for international institutions in the international environmental sphere. [83]

CONCLUSION

There is no doubt that the last three decades have seen an enormous explosion in international environmental treaty-making activity. This legislative activity has seen the further development of international environmental law and its "coming of age" as a discipline. But any analysis confined to the negotiation and conclusion of the treaty text itself will provide only part of the picture; indeed, it is but the first step on the road towards implementation and enforcement of the obligations agreed therein, obligations moreover which will evolve over time particularly in the case of treaties establishing flexible regimes. A central question following the conclusion of a treaty text remains the extent to which States implement and comply with the rules thus agreed. It is therefore not surprising to find in recent treaty texts and supplementary agreements that States are increasingly turning their attention to issues of implementation and compliance, and even to liability issues. In general these are the weakest part of international environmental law. The challenges facing environmental treaties are therefore to ensure effective implementation of existing regimes, as much as the negotiation of new substantive law. A further challenge is the relationship between treaties, and of the instruments within treaty regimes. The former will continue to arise as environmental treaties increasingly seek to rely for their implementation upon economic and other instruments, while the latter is the inevitable consequence of change within treaty frameworks.

Finally, there is the challenge which environmental treaties and environmental treaty-making pose to traditional rules of international law regarding treaty formation, adaptation, and change. The Vienna Convention on the Law of Treaties expressly takes the approach of applying without distinction to different types of treaty, be it the 1997 Treaty of Amsterdam, the 1966 International Covenant on Civil and Political Rights, or the 1982 LOSC.[84] Over the years there have been calls for the need to classify treaties in some manner, most famously perhaps by

---

82 *Op. cit.*, n.13, at p. 55.

83 See, for example, Alan E. Boyle, "Saving the World? Implementation and Enforcement of International Environmental Law Through International Institutions" (1991) 3:2 *Journal of Environmental Law*, pp. 229-245; and Sommer, *op. cit.*, n.71.

84 There are glimmers of differentiation in the VCLT, but only in Article 62(2) and in Article 20(2) and (3).

Lord McNair in the British Year Book in 1930 when he questioned whether, given the variety of functions performed by treaties, a single set of undifferentiated rules was desirable.[85] Recent literature hints at the prospect of a self-contained regime for international environmental law, insulated from *inter alia* the general provisions of the Vienna Convention. Yet examination of particular treaty regimes reveals the pervasive influence of the (residual) rules of the VCLT against which the evolution of environmental treaty texts takes place. It is premature, and possibly even undesirable, to suggest that environmental treaty-making has engendered new rules of treaty law applicable only in this sphere; rather, the dynamic development of international environmental treaties should be seen as contributing to the dynamic development of the general law of treaties.

[85] McNair, "The Functions and Differing Legal Character of Treaties" (1930) 11 BYIL, pp. 100-118. However, in its recent (and on-going) examination of reservations to treaties the ILC has clearly rejected the possibility of differentiated general rules, beyond what is already contained in the VCLT and given that the residual rules of the VCLT may always be replaced by express treaty provision.

Implementing Multilateral Treaties at the Domestic and International Levels

Chair: ERNST-ULRICH PETERSMANN

WALTER KÄLIN*

Implementing Treaties in Domestic Law: from "Pacta Sunt Servanda" to "Anything Goes"?

What is the future of international treaty law? On the one hand, treaties are still proliferating despite the fact that, at least at the multilateral level, treaty-making is becoming increasingly more difficult in a highly pluralist and heterogeneous world. On the other hand, States that traditionally have been at the forefront of strengthening the role of international law are now showing signs of growing reluctance to fully honor their treaty obligations. One aspect of this reluctance is a certain trend to avoid full implementation at the domestic level of treaty obligations deriving from multilateral treaties of a legislative character ("*traités-loi*"). National authorities in all three branches of government have developed instruments that allow their State to avoid such implementation in ways which do not technically violate international law, but that will weaken international law in the long run.

These attempts to relativize the domestic dimension of the maxim of "pacta sunt servanda" are the topic of this article. First, it presents some of the most popular ways of such avoidance. The trends and cases discussed are clear signs of the decreasing legitimacy of international law at the domestic level even in modern democratic States. Although it would be premature to speak about a legitimation crisis, it is necessary to explore the reasons for this trend. The second part of the article will analyze one important reason: how the traditional concept of separation of powers between the branches of government is being transformed into a system where national authorities collectively share their powers with actors on the international level (other States, organs of international organizations and international courts and tribunals) in a way that upsets the traditional balance of powers. In the concluding part, some possible solutions to the problem are set forth.

---

* I would like to sincerely thank Dr. Martina Caroni and Dr. Krista Nadakavukaren Schefer for their assistance in preparing and editing this article.

V. Gowlland-Debbas (ed.), Multilateral Treaty-making, 111–128.

Avoiding Treaty Implementation

The most popular among the techniques to soften the effects of ratifying an international treaty at the domestic level are: (i) the use of reservations in order to exclude new obligations going beyond those already accepted by the State concerned; (ii) the "petrification" of the original meaning of a treaty in order to exclude the possibility that subsequent developments will lead to an extended interpretation of its provisions; (iii) the exclusion of the self-executing character of the treaty without enacting implementing legislation to avoid the possibility that individuals will invoke it vis-à-vis authorities and courts in domestic procedures; and (iv) the non-publication of ratified treaties. The following discussion of these techniques draws on recent experiences in the United States and, as examples for European trends, Switzerland and Germany, i.e., countries which have been traditional promoters of a strong legal order on the international level.

Proliferation of Reservations

Most multilateral treaties allow for ratification with reservations. Reservations are unilateral statements regarding the exclusion or modification of the legal effect of specific provisions in their application to a particular State.[1] Where a treaty does not contain any clause on reservations, international law maintains that reservations are only prohibited if they are incompatible with the object and purpose of the treaty.[2] Thus, reservations facilitate a State's acceptance of a treaty in cases where the executive agrees with the purpose and content of the treaty but would find it difficult to garner a majority in the legislature for changing all domestic laws that contradict the treaty at the time of ratification. A wide acceptance of the treaty and a large number of ratifications is therefore one positive result of the availability of reservations.[3]

Despite these positive aspects, one can observe a troubling proliferation of reservations in recent times. The increasing number of reservations showing a lack of willingness to accept new obligations is particularly worrisome. The reservations by signatories to the 1966 International Covenant on Civil and Political Rights provide several pointed examples of this problem. When ratifying the Covenant in 1992, the Swiss government, for instance, entered eight reservations stripping the

---

1 See the definition of reservation in Article 2(1)(d) Vienna Convention on the Law of Treaties.

2 Article 19(c) Vienna Convention on the Law of Treaties.

3 See Human Rights Committee, General Comment 24, General comment on issues relating to reservations made upon ratification or accession to the Covenant or the Optional Protocols thereto, or in relation to declarations under article 41 of the Covenant (fifty-second session, 1994), para. 4: "The possibility of entering reservations may encourage states which consider that they have difficulties in guaranteeing all the rights in the Covenant none the less to accept the generality of obligations in that instrument. Reservations may serve a useful function to enable states to adapt specific elements in their laws to the inherent rights of each person as articulated in the Covenant".

Covenant of any legal effects going beyond those of the 1950 European Convention on Human Rights.[4] Thus, Switzerland avoided assuming any additional obligations to improve the legal status of its citizens. Even taking into account the high level of human rights protection in Switzerland, such behavior is highly problematic in the light of the principle of good faith, itself so fundamental for the law of treaties.

The same is true for the United States' ratification of the Covenant. The United States ratified the Covenant with reservations making sure that its obligations under the agreement would only extend to the degree of protection provided by the U.S. Constitution.[5] The U.S. simply modified all those provisions of the Covenant which gave better protection than constitutional law, and as a result, like Switzerland, was not required to improve the legal status of its citizens. One of the troublesome consequences of this reservation became apparent with the Supreme Court's decision that capital punishment of persons under eighteen years of age is not unconstitutional.[6] The United State's reservation to the Covenant, if valid,[7] would permit judicially-mandated death sentences of minors without any technical violation of international law, despite the nearly-universal condemnation of such practices and the codification of such condemnation in the Covenant itself. The principle of a good faith adherence to a treaty is seriously put into question by the U.S. refusal to extend its constitutional protections of the individual beyond the existing domestic regime. Such reservations, besides weakening the impact of U.S. criticism of other countries' human rights violations, damage the credibility of the Covenant as binding international law and the effectiveness of international law itself. In fact, the future of international treaty law will be dire if States continue to regularly use reservations to allow themselves the benefits of ratifying treaties without accepting any new obligations.

---

4 See Giorgio Malinverni, "Les réserves de la Suisse", in Walter Kälin, Giorgio Malinverni and Manfred Nowak, *La Suisse et les Pactes des Nations Unies relatifs aux droits de l'homme,* (2nd ed., Basel, 1997), pp. 83-104.

5 See, e.g., U.S. reservations (available at www.un.org/Depts/Treaty/final/ts2/newfiles/part_boo/iv_boo/iv_4.html) nos. 2 and 3: "(2) That the United States reserves the right, subject to its Constitutional constrains, to impose capital punishment on any person (other than a pregnant woman) duly convicted under existing or future laws permitting the imposition of capital punishment, including such punishment for crimes committed by persons below eighteen years of age. (3) That the United States considers itself bound by article 7 to the extent that 'cruel, inhuman or degrading treatment or punishment' means the cruel and unusual treatment or punishment prohibited by the Fifth, Eighth, and/or Fourteenth Amendments to the Constitution of the United States".

6 *Stanford v. Kentucky,* 492 U.S. 361 (1989).

7 See Concluding Observations of the Committee on Human Rights on the initial report of the United States of America (CCPR/C/79/Add.50, October 3, 1995), paras. 278-279 referring to General Comment 24(52). Among others, Germany, the Netherlands and France objected to the U.S. reservation regarding it as incompatible with object and purpose of the Covenant (text of objections available at www.un.org/Depts/Treaty/final/ts2/newfiles/part_boo/iv_boo/iv_4.html).

"Petrifaction" of Treaty Interpretation

"Petrified" treaty interpretation means reading the text of international agreements in the light of the original negotiators' intents without taking into account subsequent developments as required by Article 31(3) of the Vienna Convention on the Law of Treaties. The problem with such petrification is that modern treaties addressing human rights violations, environmental protection, the use of resources, or international trade and other fundamental problems of this world are "living instrument[s] which [...] must be interpreted in the light of present-day conditions".[8] Thus, evolving interpretation is necessary to maintain the effectiveness (*effet utile*) of such treaties in a world of constant change. This is one of the reasons why, according to Article 32 of the Vienna Convention on the Law of Treaties, recourse to the *travaux préparatoires* is only a "supplementary means" of interpretation.

Legislatures wanting to know the specific content of the treaty whose ratification they accept may be troubled by the rejection of negotiating history as decisive tools of treaty interpretation. Legislatures from legal systems such as the United States', where legislative history is regularly used in interpreting domestic law, may be particularly vexed by the Vienna Convention's rejection of this as a primary source of insight. But on the international level, treaties, as long-standing documents, must retain flexibility to adapt to the circumstances of the present times, not those of the original negotiators' day.

Examples of the use of a petrified reading of treaties can be found on both sides of the Atlantic. In the context of disputes over the Reagan Administration's attempt to reinterpret the Anti-Ballistic Missile Treaty, for instance, the U.S. Senate vigorously defended the position that "the United States shall interpret the Treaty in accordance with the common understanding of the Treaty shared by the President and the Senate *at the time the Senate gave its advice and consent* to ratification".[9] In Switzerland, the highest court has decided that an interpretive statement by the Federal Council on a treaty submitted to Parliament may express the Swiss position on that matter but is not legally binding.[10] In recent times, however, some Parliamentarians have clearly stated that they did not trust assurances by the Executive regarding the specific content of treaties. One example of this feeling were the debates surrounding the 1989 Convention on the Rights of the Child in 1996 where some members of Parliament wanted to block ratification with the ar-

---

[8] European Court of Human Rights, *Tyrer v. United Kingdom*, Judgment of 25 April 1978, Series A no. 26, para. 31 (regarding the interpretation of the ECHR).

[9] Biden Condition, 134 CONG.REC. 12,849 (1988) (a part of the Senate's resolution of ratification of the INF Treaty). Reprinted in Gary Michael Buechler, "Note: Constitutional Limits on the President's Power to Interpret Treaties: The Sofaer Doctrine, the Biden Condition, and the Doctrine of Binding Authoritative Representations", (1990) 78 *Georgetown Law Journal,* pp. 1983, at 1990, note 31.

[10] ATF (Federal Tribunal Decisions) 112 V 145, at 150.

gument that its content would develop over time and bind Switzerland much more than could be foreseen today.[11]

This is not the place to examine whether and to what extent legislatures are or should be entitled to impose binding interpretations on the executive or on courts. However, especially in the case of legislative treaties, the domestic implementation of international agreements will regularly run into difficulties if their meaning is evolving on the international level but has been "petrified" by the legislature for domestic purposes.

Another aspect of treaty "petrification" is the refusal of domestic courts to accept treaty interpretations by international judicial bodies which go beyond original intent. Germany provides an example here: in 1996 and 1997, a series of decisions by the European Court of Human Rights expanded the case law regarding the relevance of the prohibition of torture and inhuman treatment as embodied in Article 3 of the 1950 European Convention on Human Rights (ECHR) for aliens faced with expulsion and deportation. The European Court decided that forcibly sending an alien to another country would constitute a violation of this article not only if the person concerned would be tortured or ill-treated upon return by agents of State, but also if the danger would emanate from non-State actors or from particular situations outside the reach of States.[12] In two 1997 cases, the German Federal Administrative Tribunal rejected this expansive approach to interpretation of Article 3. The Tribunal concluded that the European Court of Human Rights had over-extended its application of the ECHR and infringed the sovereignty of State Parties to the Convention.[13] The Tribunal argued, *inter alia*, that historically the notion of torture as embodied in Article 3 ECHR was limited to acts carried out by agents of the State or attributable to the State. Therefore, it said, the interpretation given by the European Court of Human Rights not only violated the principles of interpretation as provided in Article 31 of the Vienna Convention on the Law of Treaties, but also negated the sovereign right of States to define asylum policy on their own.

---

[11] See *Bulletin officiel de l'Assemblée fédérale* 1996: Conseil National, pp. 1679; Conseil des Etats, pp. 342 and pp. 1048.

[12] In *Ahmed v. Austria*, Judgment of 17 December 1996, Reports 1996-IV, pp. 2195, the Court decided that it would be inhuman to return a refugee to Somalia where he would face torture and ill-treatment inflicted by another clan. The scope of Article 3 was even further extended by the Court in the case of *D. v. UK*, concerning the expulsion of an alien drug courier who suffered from an advanced stage of AIDS. The courier would have been returned to St. Kitts where he had no accommodation, family, moral or financial support, and no access to adequate medical treatment. The Court recognized that "[i]n view of these exceptional circumstances and bearing in mind the critical stage now reached in the applicant's fatal illness, the implementation of the decision to remove him to St. Kitts would amount to inhuman treatment by the respondent State in violation of Article 3" (Judgment of 2 May 1997, Reports 1997- III, pp. 777, paras. 52 and 53).

[13] Judgment of 15 April 1997 (EZAR 043 No. 21) and of 2 September 1997 (EZAR 043 No. 26).

Regardless of whether or not this reasoning is correct,[14] such a flat refusal to follow the case law of an international court by a domestic tribunal is highly troubling and undermines the authority of international human rights law.

Exclusion of Self-Execution

On the domestic level, treaty provisions are directly applied by courts as self-executing norms unless they need implementing legislation. In countries following the tradition of dualism, it is often the constitution which requires such transformation. In monist countries, implementing legislation is needed if the particular norm lacks justiciability, i.e., cannot be applied by courts without prior legislative action.[15] These two cases pose no problem. However, it is also possible that the legislature declares a treaty to be non-self-executing even if the agreement is suitable for direct application, and, at the same time, does not enact implementing legislation. Such declarations give rise to legitimate concerns about a State's willingness to abide by international law in any meaningful way.

The U.S. Congress has been one of the most active proponents of the use of the explicit statement of non-self-execution for avoiding full implementation of international agreements. When giving its advice and consent on the ratification not only of important trade agreements but also of human rights treaties such as the Convention against Torture or the Covenant on Civil and Political Rights,[16] Congress has frequently conditioned such approval on the insertion of language in the implementing legislation to prohibit the invocation of treaty obligations as a cause of action before the courts. As has been legitimately observed, this "raises ques-

---

[14] There are clear indications that the drafters of the ECHR did not intend to limit torture to acts of state but wanted to prohibit all forms of torture. In the Consultative Assembly of the Council of Europe the British Representative Cocks proposed to insert, in addition to what was then draft Article 2, para. 1 (guaranteeing the security of person in accordance with Articles 3,5, and 8 of the Universal Declaration of Human Rights), explicitly that "all forms of physical torture, whether inflicted by the police, military authorities, *members of private organisations or any other person*" must be prohibited (Council of Europe, Collected Edition of the *"Travaux Préparatoires" of the European Convention on Human Rights*, (The Hague, 1975), Vol. II, pp. 2 (Emphasis added). In the subsequent debate, the fact that acts of torture can be committed also by private groups and persons was taken for granted and not questioned at all. Rather, it was held that going too much into the details could limit the scope of the definition; therefore, Representative Teitgen proposed "simply to state that all torture is prohibited" (*Travaux Préparatoires,* Vol. II, p. 46. Emphasis added).

[15] See American Law Institute, Restatement of the Law Third, *The Foreign Relations Law of the United States,* Vol. 1, 1987 (American Law Institute Publishers, St. Paul, Minn.), § 111, pp. 42.

[16] For an overview of U.S. practice see Lori Fisler Damrosch, "The Role of the United States Senate Concerning 'Self-Executing' and 'Non-Self-Executing' Treaties", in Stefan A. Riesenfeld and Frederick M. Abbott (eds.), *Parliamentary Participation in the Making and Operation of Treaties, A Comparative Study* (Dordrecht/Boston/London, 1994), pp. 205, at 207-213.

tions about the seriousness of the U.S. commitment to comply with the obligations the country has assumed by ratifying these instruments".[17]
In Switzerland so far, proposals in Parliament to follow the U.S. pattern have been rejected by the majority.[18] Yet the highest Swiss court, which in general shows a positive attitude vis-à-vis the application of international law, has been unwilling to accept the self-executing character of several important treaty provisions that most agree would be suitable for direct application. These include provisions such as the prohibition of non-discrimination in Article 2(2) of the Covenant on Economic, Social and Cultural Rights[19] and the prohibition on the use of measures that are the functional equivalent of quantitative restrictions found in Article 13 of the 1972 Free Trade Agreement between the EEC and Switzerland.[20] As any implementing legislation was absent, these decisions meant that the individuals concerned remained without effective legal protection despite the fact that their government had ratified provisions which, if properly applied, would have entitled them to just such protection.

It is troubling to see how legislatures and courts reject higher standards of international law by denying direct applicability to provisions which could be applied on the domestic level without problems. Denying self-execution without enacting implementing legislation will often amount to a violation of the obligation to fulfill treaties in good faith.[21]

Non-Publication

Application of self-executing norms of a duly ratified treaty may be hindered by a delay in the publication of the instrument as required by domestic law. In practice, non-publication has the same effect as the exclusion of self-execution without implementing legislation. Thus, the Swiss Federal Tribunal expressed doubts whether the Convention on the Rights of the Child could be invoked, since at that time the text of the Convention had not yet been published.[22] Whereas, in the context of

---

[17] Thomas Buergenthal, "Modern Constitutions and Human Rights Treaties", (1997) 36 *Columbia Journal of Transnational Law,* pp. 211, at 221. See also the critical remarks in Lori Fisler Damrosch, *op. cit.,* n. 16, pp. 205-221. M. Cherif Bassiouni, "Reflections on the Ratification of the International Covenant on Civil and Political Rights by the United States Senate" (1993) 42 *DePaul Law Review,* pp. 1169-1182. Jordan J. Paust, "Avoiding 'Fraudulent' Executive Policy: Analysis of Non-Self-Execution of the Covenant on Civil and Political Rights" (1993) 42 *DePaul Law Review*, pp. 1257-1284.

[18] See *Bulletin officiel de l'Assemblée fédérale* 1984, Conseil des Etats, p. 44.

[19] ATF 121 V 246, at 250; ATF 121 V 229, at 232s.

[20] ATF 105 II 49, at 60. See Friedl Weiss, "The Functioning of the Free Trade Agreements", in Olivier Jacot-Guillarmod (ed.), *L'avenir du libre-échange en Europe: vers un Espace économique européen?* (Zurich 1990), pp. 61-78, discussing the relevant case law regarding direct applicability at 68-77.

[21] See Bassiouni, *op. cit.,* n. 17 at 1179.

[22] ATF 124 II 361, at 367.

Swiss law, this decision was wrong,[23] it would have been correct in States like France, where the Constitution grants treaties domestic force superior to legislation "upon publication"[24] or in the Netherlands where, according to the Constitution, treaties will have binding effect on the domestic level as of the time of their publication.[25]

Reasons

How can this reluctance to take treaties seriously be explained? Often domestic political factors unrelated to questions of international law will be the main reason for legislatures and executives to put obstacles in the way of effective implementation of treaty obligations at the domestic level.[26] In other cases, however, such behavior may indicate that the *legitimacy of international treaty-making is declining.* Multilateral treaty-making is often regarded by national legislators as "undemocratic" in the sense that only a few players determine the contents of treaties and that participating countries must often accept far-reaching, politically-motivated compromises that do not always reflect their interests or needs. Thus, full implementation of treaties negotiated under such conditions is less likely to occur than if the participating countries were all equally convinced of the benefit of the treaty to their self-interest. In countries such as Switzerland, where treaty law prevails over conflicting subsequent laws,[27] such feelings may be unavoidable. Thus, in order to increase their own authority, national legislators may strive to limit the effectiveness of treaties domestically through provisions affecting the treaty itself, rather than by enacting incompatible domestic legislation which would lead to international calls for accountability.

---

[23] According to a long standing principle of Swiss law, legal norms which have entered into force but have not been published, can be invoked by individuals if the provision in question grants them rights but may not be applied if it imposes obligations on them. Article 10(1) of the Swiss Law on Publication (Loi sur les publications officielles, RS 170.512) sets forth that laws and treaties impose obligations upon individuals only after their publication. See Luzius Wildhaber, *Treaty-Making Power and Constitution* (Basel/Stuttgart, 1971), at 205. Jörg Paul Müller and Luzius Wildhaber, *Praxis des Völkerrechts,* 2nd ed. (Berne, 1982), pp. 64-66.

[24] Article 55 of the 1958 Constitution.

[25] Article 93 of the 1983 Constitution.

[26] See, e.g., Louis Henkin, *Foreign Affairs and the United States Constitution,* 2nd ed. (Oxford, 1996), at 178, pointing out that often in U.S. history "the Senate denied consent not because it thought the proposed treaty was not in the national interest, but from considerations of partisan politics".

[27] This is true in principle, although there are caveats. See, e.g., ATF 99 Ib 39, at 43s. (confirming the principle but providing for an exception if Parliament adopted the later law in full knowledge of the violation of international law) and ATF 117 Ib 367, at 371 (also the European Convention on Human Rights prevails over subsequent federal laws).

Declining Latitude of Domestic Legislators

To a certain extent, this reaction has to be expected from the sharp decline of areas of "reserved domain" which can be felt by States not only in their international relations but also at the domestic level. The reach of international law into almost all aspects of domestic law is rapidly increasing and, as a consequence, national legislators may feel marginalized. Their autonomy to legislate is being limited increasingly in an interdependent world with its fast-growing body of international law. These limitations take at least three forms:[28]

1) *International law sets limitations on the autonomy of domestic law-makers to adopt new laws:* More and more often domestic law-makers find themselves in situations where their ideas or wishes cannot become law because these would violate the State's obligations already accepted under international law. In this context, the source for concern is not only the magnitude of norms which the domestic legislator had to observe but also the fact that accepted international obligations may change and expand in time. This is especially true for treaties which have entrusted an international organ with the supervision of its application. The European Convention on Human Rights provides a good example. The European Commission and Court of Human Rights have interpreted and developed the guarantees of this Convention far beyond their original meaning in many regards by stressing that the Convention is a "living instrument" to be interpreted "in the light of present-day conditions".[29] In 1988, for example, the European Court of Human Rights declared a Swiss reservation to be invalid despite its arguable compatibility with the Convention at the time of ratification.[30] A subsequent motion by the Swiss Senate to denounce the ECHR was defeated by only one vote.[31] The reason for this dissatisfaction was fairly straightforward: many senators felt that their will at the time of ratification had been disregarded by the Court and that Switzerland now was bound by obligations it had never accepted. The discussion surrounding the ratification of the Convention on the Rights of the Child revealed similar fears.[32] Treaties which institute mechanisms of control are especially likely to evolve, and thus impose expanded obligations on States, regardless of whether the control comes from such soft instruments as the discussion of country reports by treaty bodies or from

---

28 See Giorgio Malinverni, *L'indépendance de la Suisse dans un monde interdépendant, Rapports et communications de la Société suisse des juristes,* Fascicule 1, 1998, Basel 1998, pp. 1, at 42-50.

29 See *Tyrer* case, *op.cit.,* n.8.

30 European Court of Human Rights, *Belilos v. Switzerland*, Judgment of 29 April 1988, Series A no. 132. For a discussion see Luzius Wildhaber, "Parliamentary Participation in Treaty-Making, Report on Swiss Law", in Riesenfeld and Abbott, *op. cit.,* n.16, pp. 131, at 142-146.

31 See *Bulletin officiel de l'Assemblé fédérale* 1988, Conseil des Etats, pp. 554.

32 See *op.cit.,* n. 11.

quasi-judicial or judicial settlement of disputes over human rights or trade questions.

2) *International Law often obliges domestic law-makers to legislate in a specific sense*: This is not only true for most non-self-executing norms which, in general, require legislative action before they can be applied on the domestic level but may directly be imposed by a treaty provision. Thus, e.g., Article 4 of the International Convention on the Elimination of All Forms of Racial Discrimination in a rather detailed manner requires States to combat racism by enacting specific penal provisions. More generally, and leaving open much space for different solutions, international treaties may impose a whole program of legislative activities in a broad area. Thus, Article 2(1) of the International Covenant on Economic, Social and Cultural Rights obliges State Parties to take steps for "achieving progressively the full realization of the rights recognized in the present Covenant by all appropriate means, including particularly the adoption of legislative measures."[33] These and other examples show to what extent today's legislative agenda is set by international law.

3) *Legislators may be forced to change laws as a consequence of a decision of an international judicial body:* Switzerland had to change its procedural laws fundamentally in many aspects after the European Court of Human Rights had found violations of obligations under Article 6 ECHR.[34] Views of the UN Human Rights Committee led, e.g., to changes in the aliens law of Mauritius,[35] in Canada's legislation regarding indigenous peoples[36] and in the Netherlands' social security laws.[37] Such cases are still the excep-

---

[33] Similarly, the Covenant on Civil and Political Rights, in its Article 2(2) stipulates that: "Where not already provided for by existing legislative or other measures, each State Party to the present Covenant undertakes to take the necessary steps, in accordance with its constitutional processes and with the provisions of the present Covenant, to adopt such legislative or other measures as may be necessary to give effect to the rights recognized in the present Covenant".

[34] See, *inter alia*, *Minelli v. Switzerland,* Judgment of 25 March 1983, Series A no. 63 (violation of presumption of innocence by ordering an accused person to bear court costs although the criminal action had expired by the running of the statute of limitations); *Huber v. Switzerland*, Judgment of 23 October 1990, Series A no. 188 (successive exercise of the functions of investigation and prosecution by the same District Attorney in the same case); *Quaranta v. Switzerland,* Judgment of 24 May 1991, Series A no. 205 (refusal to accord free legal assistance to an accused during the investigation and at trial).

[35] Communication No. 35/1978, *Shirin Aumeeruddy-Cziffra and 19 other Mauritian women v. Mauritius,* Views adopted on 9 April 1981, Annual Report 1981, p. 134; Response, dated 15 June 1983, from the Government of Mauritius, Annual Report 1983, p. 254.

[36] Communication No. 24/1977, *Sandra Lovelace v. Canada,* Views adopted on 30 July 1981, Annual Report 1981, p. 166; Response, dated 6 June 1983, from the Government of Canada, Annual Report 1983, p. 249.

[37] See the references in Communication No. 182/1984, *F.H. Zwaan-de Vries v. the Netherlands*, Views adopted on 9 April 1987, Annual Report 1987, p. 160.

tion, but the trend goes clearly in the direction of less latitude for domestic law-makers.

It might be tempting to explain the attempts of States to reduce the impact of international law at the domestic level with this decline of the "reserved domain" only, but that would be too easy. Not only does the ratification of a treaty presuppose treaty-making power, and thus an exercise of sovereignty, but also States understand that in a highly interdependent world problems cannot be solved without international cooperation. This includes harmonization of national laws and other measures at the domestic level. In other words, the perceived decline of sovereignty is the direct *result* of the willingness of the States to accept treaty obligations in many areas – it is not the *source* of the problem discussed here.

The Separation between the Treaty-Making and the Legislative Power and its Weaknesses

In order to understand the root causes of the current problems, it is useful to recall some fundamental aspects of the relationship between international and domestic law.

International law stipulates that States must implement treaties but does not say *how* this is to be achieved on the domestic level.[38] Particularly in the case of legislative treaties ("*traités-loi*"), a tension arises between the obligation to respect and honor treaties and the freedom of States to choose the methods of domestic implementation of such treaties according to their own constitutions. This tension is not just a reflection of the inherent difficulties of overlapping legal orders; it is axiomatic for international law.

International law is more than an amalgam of traditions, politics and expediencies. It is real law and the principle of *pacta sunt servanda*[39] is one of its foundations. A second base of international law is the sovereignty of States. The same sovereignty that authorizes States to negotiate and ratify international treaties[40] allows them to shape the treaties' implementation according to domestic constitutional orders. Thus, at least in the case of modern democracies, the implementation of treaties is faced with two different logics: consensus between equal partners on the international level and government by the majority on the domestic level.

Traditionally constitutions have tried to reconcile these competing principles by clearly separating the realms of the foreign policy and domestic policy. The executive as the formal head of State is generally responsible for conducting a foreign policy. Among the executive's duties (or rather, privileges) is the initiating and negotiating of treaties with other States. The domestic policy of a State on the other hand is generally mainly under the authority of the legislature. One aspect of domestic policy is the effect of a State's international law obligations within the

---

38 Georg Dahm, *Völkerrecht* (Stuttgart, 1958), Vol. I, at 55.

39 Art. 26 Vienna Convention on the Law of Treaties.

40 See *Wimbledon Case* (1923), PCIJ Series A, No. 1, p. 25.

State. Thus, legislators also have a role in the treaty making process. Theirs is the decision whether negotiated treaties should become the "law of the land".

The separation of executive and legislative authority in the area of international treaties is best exemplified in countries following the tradition of dualism. The United Kingdom's government adheres to a nearly pure form of dualism -- all international treaty obligations that the executive (the Prime Minister in this case) accepts as binding vis-à-vis other States must be transformed into domestic law by positive Parliamentary action to enact implementing legislation.[41] In Italy,[42] while negotiation is a task of the executive, the Houses of Parliament authorize "by statute the ratification of treaties that are by their nature political", according to Article 80 of the 1948 Constitution. According to Article 10, only international customary law applies directly on the domestic level, so treaty law must be transformed by an act of Parliament.

Monist constitutions reflect the separation of executive/legislative duties in treaty-making too. In Switzerland, for instance, international obligations are generally accepted as binding on the domestic law level without any enabling legislation. Yet here too, the executive (here the Federal Council) is "generally in charge of external affairs", meaning that it is its task to determine what the negotiating position of Switzerland is in treaty-making processes. The role of the legislature (the Swiss Parliament) is to approve or reject the ratification of such treaties,[43] but there is "basically no possibility for parliament to influence the content of a draft treaty or to modify it".[44] In France "[d]uly ratified or approved treaties or agreements shall, upon their publication, override laws, subject, for each agreement or treaty, to its application by the other party".[45] There is no constitutional role for Parliament; one author has stressed that "[i]n the first place, traditionally, international relations are the privilege of the Executive. ... In the second place, Parliament has no power to interpret treaties. ... In the third place, if law conflicts with an international treaty, the French judge has the constitutional obligation to put aside the former and apply the latter. Parliament cannot, therefore, interfere with the application of a treaty."[46] The United States' attitude toward international treaty making is heavily influenced by theories of monism.[47] According to Article II, § 2 of the United States Constitution, the executive (the President in this case) has the exclusive authority to negotiate and sign treaties with other States. The constitu-

41 See The Right Honourable The Lord Templeman, "Treaty-Making and the British Parliament", in Riesenfeld and Abbott, *op. cit.*, n. 16, pp. 153-176.

42 See Giovanni Bognetti, "The Role of Italian Parliament in the Treaty-Making Process", in Riesenfeld and Abbott, *op. cit.*, n. 16, pp. 89-107.

43 Articles 166(2) and 184(2) of the 1999 Federal Constitution of Switzerland. See Wildhaber, *op. cit.*, n. 30, pp. 103.

44 Wildhaber, *op. cit.*, n. 30, p. 135.

45 Article 55 of the 1958 Constitution.

46 François Luchaire, "The Participation of Parliament in the Elaboration and Application of Treaties", in Riesenfeld and Abbott, *op. cit.*, n. 16, p. 101.

47 See Henkin, *op. cit.*, n. 26, pp. 175.

tional role of the legislature in the treaty-making process is granted to the Senate, which is permitted to give its "advice and consent" to those treaties that two-thirds of the senators wish to become part of the domestic law of the country. Whereas "advice" historically expressed the idea that "the Senate was to be a kind of Presidential council", and thus referred to an indirect involvement of lawmakers during the negotiation phase, for some time the role of the Senate has been reduced to giving its consent to the ratification of treaties as negotiated.[48]

A significant characteristic of each of these traditional models of governance is that while the legislature is *involved* in the treaty process, its members have no influence on the *content* of treaty law. Rather, the role of democratic decision-making is reduced to saying "yes" or "no" to a text negotiated by the executive. Wildhaber's description of the situation in Switzerland where "[t]here is basically no possibility for parliament to influence the content of a draft treaty or to modify it"[49] holds true for many countries. This arrangement, to a certain extent, is surprising if one takes into account that in monist countries, self-executing treaties are applied by the courts as laws, having at least the same rank as domestic (legislatively-developed) legislation or, as in Switzerland or the Netherlands,[50] even prevail over the constitution. The reduced role of the legislature in the making of treaty obligations only can be explained by a firm belief that the separation of foreign and domestic policy is warranted by the former's shaping by power relationships and the latter's by the rule of law and democracy.[51] In fact, this model has deep roots in history and it is based on a Hobbesian view of the world: if international relations are shaped by a permanent struggle over power where each of participants may militarily attack each other at any time, the very survival of the State is always at stake. Therefore, the primary duty of a government is to safeguard such survival and it must have all means at its disposal to achieve this goal. Faced with a situation of a permanent and violent struggle threatening the existence of the State, it is the responsibility of the government, as Max Weber has put it, to use all means, including immoral ones, if necessary.[52] Therefore, the government, when dealing with interstate relations cannot be bound by rules and principles which are applicable on the domestic level. If, however, States cannot afford to apply principles like democratic decision-making or the rule of law to their external relations, then a clear distinction must be made between domestic and foreign policy and the role of Parliament must, at least to a very large extent, be restricted to the former.

---

48 Henkin, *op. cit.*, n. 26, p. 177.

49 Wildhaber, *op. cit.*, n. 30, p. 135.

50 Article 191 of the 1999 Federal Constitution of Switzerland; Articles 60(3) and 63 of the Constitution of the Netherlands.

51 See on the following, e.g., Stanley Hoffman, *Duties Beyond Borders – On the Limits and Possibilities of Ethical International Politics* (Syracuse/New York, 1981), pp. 10; Walter Kälin, "Verfassungsgrundsätze der schweizerischen Aussenpolitik", *Referate und Mitteilungen des Schweizerischen Juristenvereins* 1986, Fascicule 3, pp. 269.

52 See Hoffmann, *op. cit.*, n. 51.

In 19th Century Europe, this approach has found its expression in the maxim of the primacy of foreign policy over domestic policy ("Primat der Aussenpolitik").[53]

In a world where the *ius ad bellum* has been replaced by the prohibition on the use of force (as embodied in Article 2(4) of the UN Charter) and where interstate armed conflicts have become the exception, this approach no longer reflects the realities of international relations. These realities are marked by a growing overlapping or even osmosis between international and domestic law. On the one hand, international law is harmonizing many areas which traditionally, have been the exclusive realm of domestic legislation. On the other hand, States feel a growing need to address, in their laws, problems which transcend national frontiers. In this situation, traditional models of separation of powers are no longer convincing. On the one hand, it is more and more difficult to maintain the far-reaching powers of national governments to shape foreign policy without regular recourse to parliament.[54] On the other hand, legislators have a growing feeling that they must share their powers with the international law-maker in a very one-sided manner. Whereas international law sets them important limits as described above, they cannot impact the international level. Thus, the conclusion is justified that, from a domestic perspective, the traditional power balance is severely upset in the field of treaty making and its subsequent implementation on the domestic level.

OVERCOMING THE DICHOTOMY BETWEEN FOREIGN AND DOMESTIC POLICY

What solutions could remedy this situation? When discussing domestic implementation of international treaties, it is obviously not enough to stress "the fundamental principle of international law that international law prevails over domestic law"[55] and that consequently, States must implement treaties on the domestic level in a way which ensures that they can fully comply with their international obligations. Faced with troubling developments in countries which traditionally have been at the forefront of those promoting international law as an important part of the rule of law domestically, a serious inquiry into constitutional politics is needed.

Such an approach must look for ways to remedy, or at least soften, the imbalance between the national and the international law-maker as this imbalance is one of the main reasons for the decline of international law-making's legitimacy on the

---

[53] The notion goes back to the German Wilhelm Dilthey, see Henning Behrens/Paul Noack, *Theorie der Internationalen Politik* (München, 1984), p. 98. See also the writings of Leopold von Ranke, *Politisches Gespräch* (Göttingen, 1955), pp. 60.

[54] It is true that in certain countries there might be extensive informal contacts between the government and (members of) parliament (see, e.g., Lord Templeman, *op. cit.*, n. 41, pp. 162-163 for the UK). This, however, is not true for all countries and does not solve the problem discussed here.

[55] *Applicability of the Obligation to Arbitrate under Section 21 of the United Nations Headquarters Agreement of 26 June 1947*, (*Advisory Opinion of 26 April 1988*), 1988 ICJ Rep. pp. 12, at 34, para. 57.

domestic level. Of course this cannot be done by simply transferring domestic models of democracy to the international level. Except for opening up negotiations to non-governmental organizations' participation, possibilities for meaningful democratization seem to be very limited in the context of international treaty-making. The principle that every negotiating party formally has an equal right in shaping the content of a new treaty is of paramount importance to international law and should not be diluted.

However, from a constitutional perspective, things look different. Here it is possible to open up treaty-making for democratic input, at least to a certain extent. Looking at recent developments, one can detect three approaches to make the walls between domestic and foreign policy more transparent and to allow for a certain interchange between the two levels: attempts to increase the participation of (i) parliaments in the area of foreign policy; (ii) parliamentary organs of international organizations in treaty-making; and (iii) lower levels of government in foreign policy if their interests are at stake.

Participation of Parliaments in Foreign Policy

Whereas in many States informal contacts at an early stage between the executive negotiating a treaty and the Parliament have become rather common, the new Swiss Constitution[56] contains an explicit statement to include parliamentary participation in the formation of Swiss foreign policy in general.[57] The relevance of such participation for treaty-making processes has been recognized on the level of legislation for some time. Since 1991, the law obligates the executive to consult both legislative chambers' Foreign Relations Committees on Switzerland's negotiating mandate if the treaty to be negotiated will be self-executing or if its implementation will require the enactment of legislation. During the course of negotiations, the Committees must be continuously informed and new consultations must take place if the mandate is changed.[58] The constitutional text should now provide a strong legal basis for this arrangement. As the Swiss government stressed in its report on the Draft Constitution, the motives behind this innovation are the growing interdependence of Switzerland in its external relations and the intensified effects of this process on domestic politics which have pushed Parliament to call for a more active involvement in issues of foreign policy. The new constitutional provision might be interesting as a model for other countries, too.

---

[56] On 18 April 1999, Switzerland adopted a new Federal Constitution available in German and French (on the Internet at http://www.admin.ch/ch/d/sr/c101). The idea behind the new Constitution is not to introduce any radical changes but rather to codify the existing constitutional law, including minor innovations where needed.

[57] Article 166 reads as follows: "L'Assemblée fédérale participe à la conception de la politique extérieure et surveille les relations avec l'étranger. Elle approuve les traités internationaux, à l'exception de ceux dont la conclusion relève de la seule compétence du Conseil fédéral en vertu d'une loi ou d'un traité international."

[58] Article 47bis à loi sur les rapports entre les Conseils (RS 171.11).

Participation of Parliamentarian Bodies in Treaty Making at the International Level

Some international organizations have bodies of a more or less distinct parliamentarian character that may play a role in the treaty-making process at the international level. Thus, the *European Parliament* with its directly elected members is consulted as one of the main organs of the European Union on most international agreements of the European Union with non-member States. For a limited category of treaties, its express consent is needed.[59] Despite the strong role of the Parliament, however, this model does not solve the problem of better linking the domestic and the international level, as institutionally the European Parliament has no links to national parliaments[60] and the treaties concerned are those concluded with non-member States.

More interesting is the case of the *Parliamentarian Assembly of the Council of Europe*. This assembly is made up of Representatives from each member State chosen from among the members of their national parliaments.[61] It is "the deliberative organ of the Council of Europe" and can, after debate, "present its conclusions, in the form of recommendations, to the Committee of Ministers".[62] This right includes the possibility of proposing the elaboration of treaties to be ratified by member States.[63] As such treaty-making is the most important form of standard-setting in the Council of Europe, this is an important right. However, the Assembly came to the conclusion recently that this right of initiative is not sufficient. On February 12, 1998 its Committee on Legal Affairs and Human Rights recommended an amendment to the Statute of the Council of Europe which would require the Committee of Ministers "to systematically submit all draft conventions, agreements and protocols to the Assembly for approval, prior to their adoption" and thus, to "include in the Statute the principle of co-decision in adopting conventions, agreements and protocols".[64] The explanatory memorandum stresses:

> "It is especially when a text is controversial and deals with sensitive issues that the Assembly must be consulted. What is the use of adopting international conventions which do not subsequently enter into force because they have not received a sufficient number of ratifications? Consultation with the Assembly therefore guarantees that a text will be accepted more readily by national parliaments because the parliamentarians will have been associated with it before it is adopted. Consultation of the Assembly must, therefore, rather be

---

59 Article 228(3) of the Treaty Establishing the European Community of 25 March 1957 as amended by the Treaty on the European Union of 7 February 1992.

60 In practice, however, some members of the European parliament are also members of their national parliaments.

61 Article 25 of the Statute of the Council of Europe.

62 Article 22 of the Statute of the Council of Europe.

63 Article 15 of the Statute of the Council of Europe.

64 Modification of the procedure for the adoption of Council of Europe conventions, Report of the Committee on Legal Affairs and Human Rights, Parliamentary Assembly of the Council of Europe, Doc. 8017, 12 February 1998.

considered as a preliminary step to ratification by national parliaments since, as stated in Recommendation 721(1973): 'National parliaments, which must approve a European convention before its ratification may take place, can only approve or reject the convention and have no power to amend it'."[65]

This text describes very clearly the difficult position of national parliaments and, at the same time, the possibility of improving the situation by strengthening organs of international organizations with links to these parliaments. At the time of this writing, the Committee of Ministers is considering the matter.[66] If the proposal of the Parliamentary Assembly would be approved, an interesting solution would come into existence which might inspire other organizations, too.

Participation of Local Governments in International Treaty-Making

The legitimacy of international treaty-making on the domestic level can also be enhanced by creating possibilities for local governments to participate in international treaty-making. In this sense, Belgium allows community and regional governments to conclude international treaties regarding matters within their powers.[67] The same is true for Swiss cantons.[68] Such treaties, however, concern local matters only and therefore are not very relevant for our discussion.

More important are those treaties concluded by the central government that regulate matters which directly impact on the interests of the lower levels of government. Traditionally, these governments have no right to influence the treaty-making process. This was regarded as a severe problem in federal States acceding to the European Union or ratifying its Maastricht Treaty. Therefore, the German Basic Law[69] and the Austrian Constitution[70] were amended to grant the "Länder" the right to be consulted on projects of the EU organs directly affecting their interests. Whereas these provisions are restricted to EU-matters, the new Swiss Constitution contains an article on the participation of the cantons in foreign policy in general according to which the federal government is to consult the cantons prior

[65] Explanatory memorandum to the Report, *op. cit.*, n. 64, para. 11.

[66] On 18 March 1998 the Standing Committee of the Parliamentary Assembly forwarded the proposal of the Committee on Legal Affairs and Human Rights to the Committee of Ministers (Recommendation 1361/1998). On 31 March 1998, the Committee of Ministers decided to bring the Recommendation "to the attention of their Governments" and asked their Rapporteur Group on Legal Co-operation to prepare an answer.

[67] Article 167(3) of the 1970 Constitution stipulates: "Those Community and Regional Governments described in Article 121 conclude, in matters that concern them, treaties regarding matters that are in the scope of the responsibilities of their Councils. These treaties may take effect only following approval by the council".

[68] Article 56(1) of the 1999 Constitution. On the role of Swiss cantons in foreign affairs see Nicolas Schmitt, "The Foreign Relations of Swiss Cantons", in Lidija R. Basta and Thomas Fleiner (eds.), *Federalism and Multiethnic States – The Case of Switzerland,* (Fribourg, 1996), pp. 131-175.

[69] Articles 23(5) and (6), 24(1a), 45, 50 of the 1949 Basic Law (amendments adopted in 1992).

[70] Article 23d of the 1929 Austrian Constitution (amendment adopted in 1994).

to negotiations affecting their powers or interests. In addition, the cantons are to have the possibility of directly participating in international negotiations "in an appropriate manner",[71] e.g., by having a representative as a member of the Swiss delegation negotiating the instrument.

CONCLUSION

What can be done to improve proper implementation of treaties at the domestic level? Of course, it is appropriate to remind national executives and legislatures that the principle of *pacta sunt servanda* is the foundation of international law as a legal order. Therefore, *pacta sunt servanda* must be taken seriously at the stage of domestic implementation, too, if international law is to be regarded at all. Despite the importance of widespread ratification of multilateral agreements, such a new insistence on the importance of honoring treaty obligations might lead States to more carefully consider the consequences of ratification of agreements. To be honest enough to admit, in certain cases, that the time for adherence to a particular treaty is not ripe is better both for the effectiveness of international law and the credibility of a State's own foreign policy than is ratification with many reservations and/or with declarations denying self-execution.

All of this, however, is not sufficient. At the core of the problem is the fact that the traditional dichotomy of domestic and foreign policy with the almost complete exclusion of parliaments from treaty-making no longer corresponds with the realities of today's international relations. As has been shown, there are institutional possibilities at the levels of both domestic constitutional law and the constitutions of international organizations to enhance the required osmosis between the external and domestic spheres of States in the process of treaty-making. These examples and proposals have all been developed in specific contexts and it is hardly possible to generalize them. Nevertheless, they show that it is possible to enhance the "ownership" of new treaty law on the domestic level and thus to strengthen the legitimacy of international law. It remains to be hoped that necessary reforms will be undertaken to reduce the temptation of avoiding proper implementation of ratified treaties on the domestic level.

71 Article 55 of the 1999 Swiss Constitution.

FRANCIS MAUPAIN

The ILO's Standard-Setting Action: International Legislation or Treaty Law?

INTRODUCTION

Although often described as "the old lady" of all UN Specialized agencies, the ILO is still considered to be a somewhat revolutionary organization because of its unique tripartite structure.

It is not always realized, even among those who are familiar with its Constitution and constitutional practice, that its founders' ambitions were even more revolutionary as regards the means of action which the new organization should be entrusted with. The intention of the authors of the first British draft of the Constitution was indeed to create a supranational organization capable of enacting international legislation which would have become binding subject only to an opting out clause.

Such an ambition was perfectly consistent with one of the objectives: the elimination of social dumping as reflected in one of the most famous paragraphs in its Preamble which reads as follow: "The failure of any nation to adopt humane conditions of labour is an obstacle in the way of other nations which desire to improve the conditions in their own countries". Yet, and this is interesting to note in connection with the recent debate on social clauses, this ambition was soon found unrealistic, for it would deter either membership or the adoption of truly progressive international legislation.

This intended legislative nature has, however, left its mark on international labour Conventions which, as a "product" have from the beginning assumed some of the features of an international labour "code". However, this legislative nature is even more visible with regards to the "process" of their adoption by the International Conference whose legislative prerogatives should be significantly strengthened by a recent constitutional amendment. These two aspects will be examined separately.

V. Gowlland-Debbas (ed.), Multilateral Treaty-making, 129–135.

INTERNATIONAL LABOUR CONVENTIONS AS INTERNATIONAL LEGISLATION

Once adopted by the International Labour Conference, international labour Conventions are at first sight much like other multilateral treaties. Except for Conventions concerning seafarers, they normally need two ratifications to come into force and are binding on Member States which have ratified them.

The ILO Constitution introduced however some innovations which although taken for granted today, were puzzling to international lawyers at the time of the ILO's creation:

a) The first is the fact that, in accordance with paragraph 4 of article 19 of the Constitution, Conventions are not open to signature by States but are signed *ne varietur* by the President of the International Labour Conference and the Director-General. It is worth recalling that, faced with this perplexing novelty, some countries had serious doubts about the legality of the system. An extreme example of these doubts was given by France which decided to proceed with the conclusion of bilateral agreements reproducing the text of the Conventions while at the same time opening a protocol for the signature of other Members. Fortunately, it became quickly obvious to everybody that these apparently heretic features were part and parcel of a new global *sui generis* system which had to be accepted as such.

b) The second aspect is that, once adopted without signature, international labour Conventions, even if they fail to become directly legally binding, still have some legal consequences vis-à-vis Member States, irrespective of ratification: they must be submitted to the competent authority, i.e. to the authority which has competence to legislate internally on the matter, for examination of the possibility of ratification. This provision was supplemented on the occasion of the 1946 constitutional amendment, by a new obligation placed on Member States to report to the Director-General the action taken to submit the instrument to the competent authority.

These special constitutional characteristics have led various authors to argue enthusiastically in favour of the quasi-legislative character of international labour Conventions. This view was held, in particular, by Georges Scelle who considered Conventions as international legislation (lois internationales) in the true sense of the term, and went as far as to speak of "pseudo-ratifications" to reflect the concept that ratifications *per se* did not give legal force to Conventions but simply constitute an act of accession to a legislative text.[1]

In some respects, these views may be seen as interpretations by militant lawyers who had an ideological ken to promote international integration as such. One may argue that the practice fell short of their dreams. It is interesting to note in this respect that in 1929, when the issue of the revision of Conventions was discussed

---

1 G. Scelle, *L'Organisation internationale du Travail et le BIT* (Librairie des sciences politiques et sociales, Paris, 1930), p. 183.

in the Governing Body, just about the time when Scelle published his book, the Legal Adviser of the time, Mr. Morellet, came reluctantly to the conclusion that, although Conventions had some legislative features, they still created essentially contractual obligations and that the legislative organ of the ILO, the International Labour Conference could do nothing to modify these contractual obligations unless the Conventions themselves contained enabling provisions to that effect.

In many other respects, however, the constitutional practice has lent support to a legislative interpretation of Conventions. Two aspects are worth mentioning in this respect.

The most familiar aspect of this practice is that reservations have been ruled out from the very beginning of the ILO following requests from Poland and India in 1920. The reasons, which were elaborated in more detail subsequently, are basically threefold: first, because there is a specific provision in the Constitution that the Conference itself shall consider the modifications required by the special circumstances of individual countries; secondly, because *there is no procedure for exchanging consent on reservations*; and thirdly, and perhaps most significantly, because of the tripartite character of the Conference which would make it impossible to give those involved in the adoption of the Conventions an opportunity to acquiesce in a reservation.[2]

Another consequence which has been drawn in practice, is much less known but perhaps just as significant. It relates to the interpretation of international Conventions. In theory, each instrument is a separate treaty and should be interpreted in accordance with the rules embodied in the 1969 Vienna Convention on the Law of Treaties. However, as the Office put it in its comments to the Preparatory United Nations Conference in this connection, *ILO practice recognizes a somewhat freer and more generous recourse* to the preparatory work than is envisaged by article 28 of the draft. Moreover, the object and purpose of each Convention relate to the intent of the Conference, in which Employer and Worker delegates have equal status, rather than exclusively to the intention of the parties or their subsequent agreement or practice.[3] While accurate, this statement does not give the full picture of the situation.

First, the practice to which reference is made is the practice whereby the Office and established bodies can give non-official interpretations of Conventions. The only body competent to give official interpretations is the International Court of

---

2 "Faculté de formuler des réserves dans les conventions générales", Mémorandum du Directeur du BIT, *Journal Officiel de la Société des Nations*, juillet 1927, Annexe 967a, pp. 882-884; "Written Statement of the International Labour Organisation", Memorandum by the International Labour Office, Reports of Judgments, Advisory Opinions and Orders, International Court of Justice, The Hague, 1951, pp. 216-236.

3 Statement made at the United Nations Conference on the Law of Treaties, Vienna 1968, by Mr. C. Wilfred Jenks, Principal Deputy Director-General of the International Labour Office.

Justice (ICJ).[4] It would be very interesting to see whether and how these non-official methods of interpretation would be applied if a question of interpretation was officially put to the ICJ.

Second, the scope of the practice is much broader than the Office's presentation of the issue in Vienna suggests. In concrete terms it is a fact that each Convention draws inevitably (even though not always explicitly) on concepts or even provisions developed in other Conventions. It is therefore difficult to interpret any Convention in isolation without referring more generally to the whole body of international labour standards which to that extent does constitute a fairly integrated single "legislative corpus". This last remark leads to a brief additional comment as regards "codification" of international labour Conventions. Under the title "International Labour Code", the ILO published before the war, and subsequently updated in 1951, a compilation of International labour Conventions, regrouped by subject-matter which in Wilfred Jenks words was designed "to help students who had to thread their way through a mass of unarticulated instruments, a number of which had been revised or duplicate each other".[5] This manual was however only a working tool and not a code in any proper sense of the word: more appropriate application of the concept of a code has emerged recently as a possible answer to the still growing and burgeoning mass of ILO Conventions. In order to give a clearer picture of the existing body of standards and to make the standards more understandable to outside readers, the Director-General of the ILO suggested in his report to the 1997 session of the ILC,[6] which was devoted to ILO normative action in the global economy, that they should be regrouped more systematically under the form of one global instrument covering each subject matter, which would then be open to ratification by chapter or section corresponding to previous instruments. The suggestion was overshadowed in the discussion of the ILC by other much more controversial ideas such as the proposal for "global social labelling". The discussion on the subject of regrouping is due to resume at the next session of the Governing Body (November 1998). The difficulties of the task should, however, not be underestimated. A codification of this nature requires a high degree of technicality and consistency which is difficult to maintain in a legislative process which is also a political process, the outcome of which cannot always be put into the straitjacket of legal logic, as the examination of the legislative process at the ILO will now show.

---

4 Article 37, paragraph 1, of the ILO Constitution. The Constitution of the ILO is published by the Office in a booklet entitled "The Constitution of the ILO and Standing Orders of the International Labour Conference", and is also available on the Office website <www.ilo.org>.

5 ILO: International Labour Code 1951, a systematic arrangement of the Conventions and Recommendations adopted by the International Labour Conference, 1919-1951, Geneva, 1952, 2 volumes.

6 ILO: The ILO Standard-setting and Globalization, Report of the Director-General, International Labour Conference, 85th Session, Geneva, 1997.

THE CONFERENCE AS A LEGISLATIVE BODY

Two aspects of the legislative process seem to be particularly relevant: one has to do with the concrete realities of the decision-making process as it developed and the other with a more symbolic and recent measure concerning abrogation.

Elaboration

The legislative process in the ILO rests on an interesting combination of roles and functions. The choice of a subject is the responsibility of the Governing Body of the ILO which can in this respect at least be regarded as exercising "Government" responsibilities. But once the choice is taken, the elaboration procedure combines a process of consultation of member States by the Office with a view to preparing draft texts and a process of discussion of these texts in the International Labour Conference, which is normally carried out in two successive sessions. If the process of written consultation by the Office seeks in general to elicit solutions likely to receive as general a support as possible, the process of discussion and decision at the Conference is based on majority voting.

At first sight, there is nothing very special about this. Under the Constitution, Conventions have to be adopted by a two-thirds majority,[7] which seems to represent a broad consensus but in the specific context of the ILO Constitution, it would theoretically mean that a Convention could be adopted without the support of one non-governmental group (more likely the Employers'). What is more original however is that the texts are not discussed in plenary but in tripartite committees where each group has the same voting power and where a simple majority applies. Given the group discipline which is very strong among Employers and Workers, it means that the two non-government groups can reach a majority without any government support. Alternatively (as has been the case more recently), the Workers' group can try to get the support or abstention of the majority of Governments to isolate the Employers'. When the majority exists, it is tempting in both cases to go to a vote to get a quick "progressive" solution.

There is also a time factor which plays in the same direction. The Conference has only 10 working days to deal with sometimes extremely complex issues. Even if the double discussion system gives a second chance to review and improve on the first draft, this is extremely tight. The temptation is thus very great to accelerate the process by taking votes rather than spending much time on consensus solutions. Some very complex parliamentary practice has developed, for instance the order of taking amendments (the most distant one first), which also tend to give priority to a quick result rather than to achieving an incremental progress toward a broader consensus.

This does not mean however that decision making by voting is necessarily the most expeditious system, because of the many procedural ambushes which are inherent in any parliamentary system but which tend to proliferate in a tripartite

---

7 Article 19, paragraph 2, of the ILO Constitution.

context. The power of the two groups, combined with the pressure of time, may lead to a phenomenon which can hardly be qualified as "legislative" but would rather partake of a form of "international collective bargaining". The two groups meet informally to iron out their divergences and the plenary committee has little choice but to adopt the solution agreed behind the scenes. This is especially true in the case of maritime instruments. Maritime Sessions of the Conference are rather infrequent, and well-organized shipowners' and seafarers' unions are generally keen to get as much as they can from them.

There is however a price to pay for this specific and more expeditious way of conducting business. The price is first that the "travaux préparatoires" are lacking in clarity on the meaning of solutions which have been agreed behind the scenes and are sometimes deliberately – more or less – not really intelligible. But more seriously, the fact that a Convention whose provisions have been adopted in committee on the basis of a simple majority, even if it gets a two-third majority at the final vote, does not necessarily command sufficient positive support to be widely ratified by Governments.

The decrease in ratifications is detrimental to the credibility of Conventions and led the Director-General of the ILO to plead repeatedly in favour of a shift of emphasis in standard setting from Conventions to Recommendations. This argument has so far been strongly resisted by the Workers as they claim that Conventions, even not ratified, exercise an influence, especially on national collective bargaining. Although this influence is certainly true, the argument is a bit circular as Recommendations are precisely designed to exercise an influence without the ratification process. The real reason is that international labour Conventions have the higher prestige which attaches to putative international labour legislation. The result is however, that the ILO normative corpus contains a certain number of still-born instruments which in some cases have become obsolete before entering into force.

Abrogation

Recent measures permitting the abrogation of obsolete Conventions provide a powerful symbolic message concerning the legislative nature of ILO Conventions. It should be noted first that international labour legislation bears on a rather volatile and unstable matter. In the field of labour, realities and approaches vary sometimes quickly and require adjustments to the content of the standards. Very shortly after the adoption of the first Conventions, in the twenties, it became clear that they would require adjustments if they were to remain relevant. The question was, however, what to do about Conventions already ratified which the Conference considered ill-adapted. As indicated above, the Legal Adviser of the time, Mr. Morellet, while paying lip-service to its "legislative" character, concluded that, because of the contractual aspect inherent in the ratification process, the Conference had no power at least in the Constitution as it then existed, to modify the obligations arising out of these ratifications. The only way out therefore was to insert in the final provisions of future Conventions a clause providing that the ratification of the new

Conventions would involve the automatic denunciation of the earlier one and that the entry into force of the new Convention would close the earlier one to any future ratifications.

While extremely useful, this solution proved not to be quite sufficient in the long run. It could do nothing about Conventions adopted prior to 1929 which were increasingly found obsolete but continued to create legal obligations and a potential administrative burden on States and the Organization for no valid purpose. In addition, for Conventions subsequent to 1929, the only way to keep a Convention on any particular matter up-to-date was to pile up one revision after another without being able to automatically eliminate the legal effects of the earlier texts with regard to member States who may not be prepared either to denounce them or to ratify the revised text.

This is the reason why, as recently as 1997, the Governing Body and the Conference finally opted for the rather drastic solution of a Constitutional amendment which gives the Conference the power to abrogate, *vis-à-vis* the ILO, all legal effects of Conventions which the Conference deems obsolete: i.e. not serving any longer any useful purpose for the promotion of ILO objectives.[8]

More than any other aspect, this development would seem to consolidate the legislative interpretation of the International Labour Conference as an organ capable of adopting and repealing international legislation in the light of its ability to achieve the permanent objectives of the Organization. It is significant that the consideration which seems to have been decisive in the adoption of this amendment, is that Conventions are not to be regarded as ends in themselves but rather, like laws, as legal tools whose "raison d'être" is subordinated to the more general and fundamental objectives spelled out in the Constitution.

In the same perspective, another development seems worth mentioning in conclusion. It relates to the adoption by the Conference in June 1998 of a Declaration on Fundamental Principles and Rights at Work. This Declaration spells out fundamental principles and rights which all Members of the ILO, whether or not they have ratified corresponding international labour Conventions, recognize they have to promote as an expression of the fundamental values and objectives they have accepted in joining the Organization. This Declaration cannot be regarded as an interpretation of the Constitution because the Conference is not competent to interpret the Constitution. It could rather be seen as a form of quasi-legislative pronouncement directly based on the Constitution which all Members have accepted in advance to follow as such.

---

[8] ILO: *Records of Proceedings*, International Labour Conference, 85th Session, Geneva, 1997, Nos. 1 and 10; pp. 248-250 and p. 304; ILO: *Official Bulletin*, Series A, 1997, Vol LXXX, No. 2, pp. 77-78.

GEORGES ABI-SAAB

Concluding Remarks

Two years ago, the title of our first joint Geneva Forum was *"The Proliferation of International Tribunals"*. But its real theme and subject of debate was the impact of such proliferation on the unity and coherence of the international legal system and how to preserve them in spite of the continuing demand for specialized jurisdictions in response to the growing complexity of, and diversification of needs within, the international environment. This is not without recalling the subject-matter of today's Forum, which is another variation on the theme of unity and diversity in international law, namely how can we develop international law in response to the increasing complexity and diversity of international life, while preserving its central unity and what is the role of multilateral treaties in this process.

This "problematic" is not new. Indeed, multilateral treaties as legal instruments made their appearance in the 19th Century at a time of rapid technical change, as the industrial revolution was taking off. Used for the first time in The Final Act of the Congress of Vienna[1] the multilateral treaty was perceived as an instrument of legislation allowing for conscious and sophisticated legal regulation of complex activities made possible by technical progress, such as the railways and the telegraph, which can operate at a scale transcending any one state, but require for that the co-operation and the adoption of common standards by all States involved; whence the nomenclature, "*traité-lois*".

The nomenclature reveals, however, a hiatus between the means and the end. For notwithstanding their "legislative" aspiration, as a response to the need for general or universal rules, multilateral treaties remain in essence contractual, hence "relative" instruments, binding only on those States that become parties to them. They are thus unable, by themselves, to effect general legal regulation, i.e. legislation.

[1] For the origins and history of multilateral treaties, see Manfred Lachs, "Le développement et les fonctions des traités multilatéraux" (1957-II) 92 *Recueil des cours,* p. 229; Paul Guggenheim, "Contribution à l'histoire des sources du droit des gens" (1958-II) 94 *Recueil des cours,* p. 1 at 70 ff.

V. Gowland-Debbas (ed.), Multilateral Treaty-making, 137–142.

At the end of the 20th century, this problem is still with us as has clearly appeared from today's discussions on the role of multilateral treaties in "the international legislative process". The discussions also revealed that, in the contemporary process of development of international law, this dilemma is compounded by another one, namely, how to accommodate the clear centrifugal tendency towards diversification and specialization in response to the growing complexity of international life with the countervailing need for common general rules in order to maintain the unity of the international legal system.

Our discussions of these dilemmas in relation to "multilateral treaty making" revolved around three axes: its process, fora, and outcomes; as well as two sources of complexity: the multiplicity of actors and the heterogeneity of subject-matters.

THE PROCESS

Can we really speak of an "international legislative process", or should we call it a "quasi-legislative process"? I have argued elsewhere that the international community has managed to develop, in and around the UN, a "legislative process", but without managing to impart it with "legislative power" or "effect".[2]

What is the substance of this process? Do we define it by the nature of the activity, or by its final product? Alain Pellet, as the title of his presentation reveals – *"Responding to new needs through codification and progressive development"* – started by putting the emphasis on the nature of the activity. But the formula of Article 13 of the Charter is quite flexible, accommodating a very wide spectrum. It stretches from "codification" *stricto sensu* – i.e. a faithful written rendering or snapshot of customary law as it exists, which is a pure fiction because by writing unwritten law it becomes fundamentally different – to "progressive development" which ranges from elaborating, completing, updating and systematizing existing law to formulating new law for new situations, i.e. legislation *stricto sensu*..

Anyway, Professor Pellet ended up adopting the other definition of the process, not as a function of its input, (whether there is, and how much, pre-existing law), but of its desired output, i.e., the production of a code, a complete legal regulation of a whole subject-matter.

The question of process becomes then how to beget complete and coherent bodies of legal regulation of general application as to their personal reach, though they may deal *ratione materia* with a special subject or field.

---

[2] Georges Abi-Saab, "Cours général de droit international public" (1987-VII) 207 *Recueil des cours*, p. 179.

THE FORA

The answer to this question largely depends on the forum within which the process takes place.

Professor Pellet suggests that, as far as the general part or aspects of international law are concerned, the Sixth Committee of General Assembly (which chooses the subjects and thus decides the "needs"), together with the International Law Commission (which undertakes the technical work of rationalizing the material and formulating the drafts), possibly followed by codification conferences, bring this process a good part of, if not all, the way towards a "legislative" process. But the province of this "ILC *cum* 6th Committee" process is limited, according to Prof. Pellet, to the general aspects of international law.

For him, the main task of the ILC is to guarantee the unity of general international law, the law of the international community, and to respond to its constant and renewed needs for general rules. But it is not suitable for responding to more particular needs in technical fields which should be left to more specialized fora to deal with.

Indeed, technical subjects call for tighter and more "legislative", in the substantive sense of *ex nihilo*, regulation; hence more "legislative" in the procedural sense (or more akin to internal legislation) as well. Such hybrid process can be formal in the specialized fora that deal with these matters such as the International Telecommunications Union, the World Health Organization and the International Labour Organization to which Mr. Maupain referred earlier today. Even so, these processes always contain an escape (or "opting out") clause.

The international community has thus developed various international legal processes, but it never managed to attribute full legislative effect to them. The final product that comes out of the assembly line does not have automatically the status of legislation. There is a hiatus here, and this hiatus has to be filled somehow.

THE OUTCOMES

Let us suppose now that after a hard day's work, a multilateral treaty is concluded, which resembles a piece of legislation covering all the aspects of a subject-matter in a general, forward-looking manner. What, then, is the *outcome?*

A treaty *qua* treaty binds only those States that ratify it, and takes a long time to be formally accepted by a large number of them. There are only few multilateral treaties with very wide or all encompassing participation such as the Geneva Conventions of 1949 and the Charter of the United Nations. According to Charles Brower, in many cases, States do not feel the need to ratify an already widely accepted multilateral treaty, because they consider it as having become general international law or otherwise acquired the status of custom. He also stated, however, that such status cannot be assumed. In my opinion, law-making multilateral treaties, if they perdure, i.e. demonstrate their staying power, would in fact structure expectations. And if they structure expectations, they have become general international law – whatever the theoretical explanation. And the doctrine of the persistent objector would not hold there. No state can stay out of a general rule for a very long time; it either breaks the rule while it is in the making or the rule, once firmly established, breaks its objection. But the problem remains, as far as procedural rules and institutional mechanisms are concerned. For while essential for the effective regulation of highly sophisticated regimes dealing with new and technical subjects, theses rules do not pass easily (in fact not at all) into custom.

A comment on *Soft Law* as a possible alternative outcome is here in order. Proceeding from the Roman Law distinction between the *"negotium"* and the *"instramentum",* soft law instruments (General Assembly normative resolutions, non-binding agreements), are not "binding" by themselves. Their legal standing in international law may be analogous to unratified treaties or treaties with limited ratifications vis-à-vis third parties. But soft law is very important in its own right, because it fulfils several functions and Professor Bruno Simma discussed some of them. One such function is that soft law expands "law's empire" into new areas by laying the groundwork for subsequent developments.

This is not to say, however, that soft law is merely law "in the making". It can be a different type of legal regulation and thus poses different problems of implementation. Indeed, the more diverse the situations and the more complex the issues in a subject, the more likely it is that obligations stipulated for its regulation are couched in the form of obligations of "best efforts" – i.e. "obligations de moyen" – and obligations of best efforts stretched to the extreme merge into soft law. Classical international law is full of obligations of result; they were simply obligations of forbearance or abstention, a cardinal virtue in the law of co-existence. The law of co-operation, on the other hand, entails obligations of performance or action (obligations de faire) which can hardly be obligations of result – since no specific result can be guaranteed before hand. They are largely obligations of best efforts, as far as the results are concerned. The law of the environment, in which responsibility operates somewhat differently from other fields of international law more imbued with the "law of co-existence" approach, is a case in point.

The distinction between hard law and soft law is not always clear-cut. The formulation of normative propositions and their reiteration and reflections in practice would ultimately structure expectations, through a cumulative process, inching these propositions towards the threshold of law.

THE MULTIPLICITY OF ACTORS

What accounts for the complexity of the process and its outcomes just noted? One factor is the multiplicity of *actors*. Previously, there were only States and their plenipotentiaries exercising full powers and, when negotiating a treaty, it is only their actions that were taken into consideration. For this reason, it was seen as something of a novelty when, in the Norwegian Fisheries case, the International Court of Justice alluded to the behaviour of fishermen. But today, not only do States themselves exhibit differences and heterogeneity – in terms of composition of their constituent communities, culture and world visions, as well as the way in which they understand the word "law" – but there are also non-state actors, such as the ICRC, (which is nearest to a public authority, as it is imparted with an international mandate), as well as other NGOs and, thanks to the phenomenon of globalization, transnational corporations have been added to the list. Since the 1960s, there have been discussions on the possibility of a two-tier legal regulation in which States would be asked to control those non-State entities operating within their respective jurisdictions. It has not yielded much effect, however, because some of these actors, the transnational ones, could not be pinned down in any one state. According to Charles Brower, there are two strategies available today to the international community: the first is to "contract out" the regulation to the actors themselves, i.e. its "privatization", but the effectiveness of regimes based on mere self-regulation by the interested parties is highly doubtful; the other, and in my opinion more desirable, is to effect the regulation at the level of the phenomenon, i.e., on the international plane, an imperative which is rendered more urgent with the acceleration of the process of globalization.

THE SPECIFICITY OF SUBJECT-MATTERS

Another factor that explains the complexity of outcomes concerns the specificity of particular subject-matters which the international community seeks to regulate. Human rights law and the law of the environment, for instance, both elicit a special type of regulation consonant with their subject-matter.

But we can also add from recent experience the Law of the Sea, International Trade Law, etc. In some of these cases, and to some extent, the specificity emanates from the nature of the subject matter; but in others, it is specificity by design. In all cases, however, whatever the special regulation sought, it has to be effected within the framework of general international law and in conformity with its basic principles. In other words, it has to have its anchorage in general international law, as there can be no totally self-contained regimes in international law – (or in any legal system for that matter).

I would like to end these disparate reflections on our debates by drawing two transversal or across the board conclusions.

To the question or the dilemma of how to accommodate the increasing demand for, and trend towards diversity with the imperative of preserving the unity of the international legal system, the answer that emerges seems to be that we have to use whatever instruments currently available – be they multilateral treaties or normative resolutions – in order to build "general" frameworks within the parameters of the legal system but without going too far in the details, in order to avoid the trap of "over regulation" or "micro-management" on the general level. The details can be worked out by other means, such as the specification of the general principles through State practice, particularly in internal legislation, or by concluding additional international instruments where it is difficult to obtain consensus on very specific rules at one go. For instance, negotiations on the Law of the Sea started with a resolution on one issue, namely the status of the sea bed beyond national jurisdiction in 1967, and continued for a decade and a half, before yielding a mammoth convention covering the whole range of issues which entered into force just two years ago.

The other conclusion relates to the question of how to ensure the continuity between international regulation and internal implementation. In this respect I think we should consider the relationship between international law and municipal law in a new light.

We are used to a static model of the State, but the State is in the process of transmutation – its pores are widening to allow for more intensive interaction with its environment. A good example is the inclusion in one way or another of non-State actors at recent multilateral negotiations. The way in which social needs have been addressed by States should be reinforced through a kind of democratic participation, and for this reason I agree with Professor Kälin that the dichotomy between the two schools of monism and dualism is somewhat artificial today. States should devise ways and means whereby a final decision adopted at the international level may be applied adequately within their jurisdictions. Some might say, perhaps, that the most progressive way is absolute monism; but even so, the process through which rules of international regulation are formulated is such that internal judges may not fully understand them. More appropriate would therefore be a system of conscious transformation of international norms into municipal law – one which is not necessarily dualist in nature but inspired from federalism, and which would guaranteed their ultimate application in the internal fora.

List of Participants

Georges ABI-SAAB	Professor of Public International Law, Graduate Institute of International Studies; Member of the Institute of International Law
Alan BOYLE	Professor of Public International Law, Faculty of Law, University of Edinburgh
Charles N. BROWER	Past President, American Society of International Law; Judge, Iran-United States Claims Tribunal; Partner, White & Case LLP; formerly Acting Legal Adviser, United States Department of State; Deputy Special Counsellor to the President.
Andrew CLAPHAM	Associate Professor of Public International Law, Graduate Institute of International Studies, Geneva
Louise DOSWALD-BECK	Head of the Legal Division, International Committee of the Red Cross
Vera GOWLLAND-DEBBAS	Professor of Public International Law, Graduate Institute of International Studies, Geneva
Larry JOHNSON	Legal Advisor, International Atomic Energy Agency
Walter KÄLIN	Professor of International and Constitutional Law, Faculty of Law, University of Bern

Peter MALANCZUK	Professor of International Law, Faculty of Law, Erasmus University, Rotterdam; Director Institute of Globalization, International Economic Law and Dispute Settlement (GLODIS-Institute); Honorary Professor, Peking University, Counsel, Lalive & Partners, Geneva
Francis MAUPAIN	Legal Advisor, International Labour Organization
Stephen MCCAFFREY	Professor of International Law, McGeorge School of Law, University of the Pacific
Alain PELLET	Professor, Université de Paris X-Nanterre and Institut d'Etudes Politiques de Paris; Member and Former Chairman, International Law Commission
Ernst-Ulrich PETERSMANN	Professor of International and European Law, University of Geneva and Graduate Institute of International Studies
Catherine REDGWELL	University Lecturer and Yamani Fellow in Public International Law, St Peter's College, University of Oxford
Robert ROSENSTOCK	Member of the International Law Commission
Bruno SIMMA	Professor of Public International Law, University of Munich; Member, International Law Commission

NIJHOFF LAW SPECIALS

1. D. Campbell: *Abortion Law and Public Policy.* 1984 ISBN 90-247-3107-0
2. J. Pictet: *Development and Principles of International Humanitarian Law.* 1985 ISBN 90-247-3199-2
3. J. van Houtte: *Sociology of Law and Legal Anthropology in Dutch-speaking Countries.* 1985 ISBN 90-247-3175-5
4. C.D. De Fouloy: *Glossary of NAFTA Terms.* 1994 ISBN 0-7923-2719-5
5. H.L. Zielinski: *Health and Humanitarian Concerns.* Principles and Ethics. 1994 ISBN 0-7923-2963-5
6. K.S. Foster and D.C. Alexander: *Prospects of a US-Chile Free Trade Agreement.* 1994 ISBN 0-7923-2885-X
7. F.J.M. Feldbrugge (ed.): *Russian Federation Legislative Survey. June 1990-December 1992.* 1995 ISBN 0-7923-3243-1
8. R. Platzöder (ed.): *The 1994 United Nations Convention on the Law of the Sea.* Basic Documents with an Introduction. 1995 ISBN 0-7923-3271-7
9. D. Warner (ed.): *New Dimensions of Peacekeeping.* 1995 ISBN 0-7923-3301-2
10. M. van Leeuwen (ed.): *The Future of the International Nuclear Non-Proliferation Regime.* 1995 ISBN 0-7923-3433-7
11. E.-U. Petersmann: *International and European Trade and Environmental Law After the Uruguay Round.* 1995 ISBN 90-411-0857-2
12. V. Gowlland-Debbas: *The Problem of Refugees in the Light of Contemporary International Law Issues.* 1996 ISBN 90-411-0085-7
13. A. Kaczorowska: *International Trade Conventions and Their Effectiveness.* Present and Future. 1995 ISBN 0-7923-3362-4
14. T.F. Acuña: *The United Nations Mission in El Salvador.* A Humanitarian Law Perspective. 1995 ISBN 90-411-0123-3
15. H. Wiggering and A. Sandhövel (eds.): *European Environmental Advisory Councils.* 1996 ISBN 90-411-0873-4
16. E.A. Ankumah: *The African Commission on Human and Peoples' Rights.* Practice and Procedures. 1996 ISBN 90-411-0130-6
17. B. de Rossanet: *Peacemaking and Peacekeeping in Yugoslavia.* 1996 ISBN 90-411-0192-6
18. A. Webster and K. Packer (eds.): *Innovation and the Intellectual Property System.* 1996 ISBN 90-411-0907-2
19. H. Bocken and D. Ryckbost (eds.): *Codification of Environmental Law.* Draft Decree on Environmental Policy. 1996 ISBN 90-411-0911-0
20. K. Lescure and F. Trintignac: *International Justice for Former Yugoslavia.* The Working of the International Criminal Tribunal of the Hague. 1996 ISBN 90-411-0201-9
21. G. de Nooy (ed.): *The Role of European Naval Forces after the Cold War.* 1996 ISBN 90-411-0227-2
22. M. Bertrand and D. Warner (eds.): *A New Charter for a Worldwide Organisation?* 1997 ISBN 90-411-0286-8

NIJHOFF LAW SPECIALS

23. E.-U. Petersmann: *The GATTWTO Dispute Settlement System.* International Law, International Organizations and Dispute Settlement. 1996 ISBN 90-411-0933-1
24. G. de Nooy (ed.): *Cooperative Security, the OSCE, and its Code of Conduct.* 1996 ISBN 90-411-0316-3
25. M. Bertrand: *The United Nations.* Past, Present and Future. 1997 ISBN 90-411-0337-6
26. D. Dijkzeul: *The Management of Multilateral Organizations.* 1997 ISBN 90-411-0356-2
27. G. de Nooy (ed.): *The Role of European Ground and Air Forces after the Cold War.* 1997 ISBN 90-411-0397-X
28. M. Hilaire: *International Law and the United States Military Intervention in the Western Hemisphere.* 1997 ISBN 90-411-0399-6
29. D. Warner (ed.): *Human Rights and Humanitarian Law.* The Guest for Universality. 1997 ISBN 90-411-0407-0
30. J.C. Hathaway (ed.): *Reconceiving International Refugee Law.* 1997 ISBN 90-411-0418-6
31. G. de Nooy (ed.): *The Clausewitzian Dictum and the Future of Western Military Strategy.* 1997 ISBN 90-411-0455-0
32. Canadian Council on International Law and The Markland Group (ed.): *Treaty Compliance: Some Concerns and Remedies.* 1997 ISBN 90-411-0732-0
33. B. de Rossanet: *War and Peace in the Former Yugoslavia.* 1998 ISBN 90-411-0499-2
34. C.M. Mazzoni (ed.): *A Legal Framework for Bioethics.* 1998 ISBN 90-411-0523-9
35. M. Marín-Bosch: *Votes in the UN General Assembly.* 1998 ISBN 90-411-0564-6
36. L. Caflisch: *The Peaceful Settlement of Disputes between States: Universal and European Perspectives. Règlement pacifique des différends entre États: Perspectives universelle et européenne.* 1998 ISBN 90-411-0461-5
37. R. Wazir and N. van Oudenhoven (eds.): *Child Sexual Abuse: What can Governments do?* A Comparative Investigation into Policy Instruments Used in Belgium, Britain, Germany, the Netherlands and Norway. 1998 ISBN 90-411-1034-8
38. E.M. Barron and I. Nielsen (eds.): *Agriculture and Sustainable Land Use in Europe.* 1998 ISBN 90-411-9691-9
39. K. van Walraven (ed.): *Early Warning and Conflict Prevention.* 1998 ISBN 90-411-1064-X
40. S. Shubber: *The International Code of Marketing of Breast-milk Substitutes.* An International Measure to Protect and Promote Breast-feeding. 1999 ISBN 90-411-1100-X
41. G. Prins and H. Tromp (eds.): *The Future of War.* 2000 ISBN 90-411-1196-4
42. Choung Il Chee: *Korean Perspectives on Ocean Law Issues for the 21st Century.* 2000 ISBN 90-411-1301-0
43. K. Idris and M. Bartolo: *A Better United Nations for the New Millennium.* The United Nations System – How it is now and how it should be in the future. 2000 ISBN 90-411-1344-4

NIJHOFF LAW SPECIALS

44. E. McWhinney: *The United Nations and a New World Order for a New Millennium.* Self-determination, State Succession, and Humanitarian Intervention. 2000 ISBN 90-411-1371-1
45. C.Y. Pak: *Korea and the United Nations.* 2000 ISBN 90-411-1382-7
46. V. Gowlland-Debbas (ed.): *Multilateral Treaty-making.* The Current Status of Challenges to and Reforms Needed in the International Legislative Process. 2000 ISBN 90-411-1448-3

MARTINUS NIJHOFF PUBLISHERS – THE HAGUE / BOSTON / LONDON